FOUR QUARTERS

D. RAY BOOKER

PREFACE

Many years ago, I became curious about who my ancestors were, what they did and how they lived. My Grandpa Booker, who was a great storyteller, related many colorful and interesting stories about his childhood beginning during the Civil War in Tennessee. Unfortunately, none of what he knew was ever written down. Years after he died, I decided to learn more about him and where our family came from. As I began digging through old census records, military logs and other old documents I compared my recollection of what Grandpa said and what Dad could remember against the available records. The old documents recorded births, deaths and marriages, but they did not tell me what kind of people my ancestors were, how they lived and why they did the things they did. I wished that my ancestors had written something about themselves for the benefit of later generations. I became convinced that every person should leave some record of their lives so their great grandchildren can have some idea who they are and where they came from. This is my attempt at creating such a record.

IN HONOR OF MY MOTHER

My mother was the most important person in my life. She was always there for me with unconditional love, support and guidance. Her faith and strength, patience, persistence and hard work kept our family together during some difficult times. She departed this life with the same strength, courage and grace with which she lived. This book is dedicated to her memory and it is meant to honor her.

My mother on her 90th birthday

FIRST QUARTER – GROWING UP

BACKGROUND AND EARLY YEARS

Grandpa and Grandma Booker

Grandpa Booker grew up on a Tennessee farm that had been carved out of the wilderness by his great grandfather, John Booker. In about 1798, John Booker moved from Virginia to settle in east Tennessee. He acquired about 600 acres straddling Little Flat Creek, about two miles downstream from what is now Luttrell. The farm was about 20 miles northeast of a small settlement called Knoxville. He built a stout two-room log house and began developing the farm. He died in 1803. John and his wife, Elizabeth, were buried in a small family cemetery on top of a hill about a half mile from the log house.

The second of John's eight children, George, inherited the Booker farm. In about 1820, he doubled the size of the log house to four rooms, two upstairs and two downstairs. The house still has the same four rooms today and is in reasonably good shape. Nicholas, the sixth of George's twelve children, was born at the farm in 1833.

In 1859, Nicholas married Mary Ann Webster, the daughter of Sanders Webster, a successful farmer from nearby House Mountain. Sanders had six daughters and only one son, so Nicholas helped run the Webster farm before and after the Civil War.

Nicholas and three brothers joined the Union Army in 1861. Nicholas was wounded and was hospitalized in Knoxville. An affidavit by the doctor who attended him in death stated that Nicholas believed his wound contributed to pericarditis, which was the cause of his death.

In October 1879, Nicholas sold his part of the Booker farm to his brother James for $400, and then joined a wagon train moving west. By that time, Nicholas' family had grown to eight children, ranging from one year old Sherman to 17 year old William Thornburgh (Grandpa). In the fall of 1879, he settled his family on a rented farm in a rugged, heavily wooded area a few miles southeast of Willow Springs in Howell County, south central Missouri.

Mary Ann, age 43, died at the farm less than a year later in September 1980. Nicholas, age 48, died five months later. Both were buried in the Moffitt Cemetery, just southeast of Willow Springs, with simple sandstone markers bearing no names. Eight orphaned children were left to fend for themselves. Dr. Moffitt, who treated Nicholas during his final illness, met with the children and arranged for the younger children to be distributed among sympathetic neighbors to be raised. Dr. Moffitt adopted 2 year old Sherman.

Grandpa, his brother, George and Julian Hickle, a cousin, became involved in some sort of fight with what Grandpa called "them ___ carpetbaggers" in about 1884. Although Grandpa never talked about the details of the fight, one result was that Grandpa, George and Julian confiscated a horse drawn carnival from the "carpetbaggers" and made a hasty one-way trip to the Indian Territory. They sold the carnival in Sallisaw and bought some cattle. Grandpa did not (could not) return to Missouri for several years.

Grandpa was a great storyteller. He told of climbing a mountain that he called "Lookout Mountain" with his mother and grandmother to watch a Civil War battle in the valley below. He described how the two armies came together in a field, and were engulfed in smoke as the battle broke out. He said he could see riderless horses running out of the smoke cloud from time to time.

Grandpa counted Sam and Bell Starr, and Sam's brother Pony among his friends in the Indian Territory. He said he went to a dance held at a house at Briartown the night Sam Starr was shot. He was standing on the porch when Sam and Belle Star drove up in a buggy. Just as Sam stepped out of the buggy, someone shot and killed him. Belle grabbed a gun and began shooting. The battle lasted most of the night. The next morning, there were several dead people around the house and barn. Dad said Grandpa pointed to the house as they drove through

Briartown one day and remarked that the house looked about the same as it did the night of the big battle. Grandpa also told of standing on the dock of the train depot in Sallisaw when some outlaws stepped off the train and got into a gunfight with other outlaws who were waiting for them. Mom told me that Grandma sometimes told her that Grandpa had lots to make up for, referring to his younger days in the Indian Territory.

Grandpa rode the shotgun seat on a stagecoach line between Muskogee and Fort Smith for a while. The stagecoach often transported money belonging to the Cherokees. He said that nobody would hold up the stagecoach and steal money from the Indians because their revenge would be swift and sure.

Grandpa married Susan Vermell Fry in 1888 at Fort Smith. Shortly after that, they returned to Missouri to be near his brothers and sisters. He evidently rented a farm there. He was the secretary of the Southwest Missouri Anti-Horse Thief Association. He told me that he and other association members rode to Bald Knob, Arkansas to recover a herd of stolen horses. He said they got into a gunfight with the "baldknobbers" but they did recover most of the stolen horses.

Grandpa and his brother, George, trained a horse for six months so Grandpa could ride him in the Run of '89 into the Cherokee Strip. He put his flag down on a claim. He said nothing was on it but dry grass, with no water as far as he could see. He traded his claim for a gold watch and returned to the farm in Missouri.

He moved his growing family to a farm near Sallisaw, Indian Territory in about 1894. He eventually moved to a farm near Nocona, Texas where they lived for several years. Dad was born there in June 1909.

By 1912, all of the land around Nocona, Texas was developed and fenced. Although Grandpa's farm was prosperous, he wanted access to open (free) range land for his cattle and hogs. He and his brother, George, drove a buggy north across the Red River, searching for a new home. After looking at many farms across southern Oklahoma, they found a 160 acre farm for sale at Hall Community, about 5 miles southwest of Antlers. Several square miles of open rangeland were immediately west and northwest of the farm. The land was producing 40-50 bushels of corn per acre. The farm had good rail fences over most of it. The family moved into the existing rough two-story house near the northwest corner of the farm. Grandpa later built a new house on the top of a hill along the north side of his farm where he could see the entire farm from his back porch. Grandpa was 55 years old when Randal Weldon "Pete," the last of his 12 children, was born at the Antlers farm in 1916.

Hall School, a one-room schoolhouse for grades one through eight, was just across the road north from Grandpa's new house. An additional room was later added to the schoolhouse. It served as a community church on Sundays. It was still a two room school and church when I finished the 8th grade there.

Grandpa and Grandma Booker at Hall about 1936.

Grandma Booker was a deeply religious woman who always worked very hard at cooking, gardening, mending clothes and taking care of a large family of boys. She suffered severe bouts of asthma all of her life. While living at Antlers, a doctor told Grandpa and Grandma that her asthma would be less severe in a drier climate. Because of that advice, Grandpa moved the family to Greer County in western Oklahoma in 1927 in hopes that Grandma's asthma would improve. However, they never liked western Oklahoma. Grandpa complained that there was nothing there but jackrabbits and wind. Life was difficult there even in good years. That was a time of economic depression, protracted drought and severe dust storms in western Oklahoma. Most Greer County farmers lost their farms and were forced to pack up and move elsewhere in search of a better life. Grandma missed her church, her garden and her orchard that she had at Hall Corner.

The dust made Grandma's breathing problems worse than they had been at Antlers. Grandma insisted they move back to the Antlers farm, which they did in 1935. Grandma died there in 1938.

Grandpa farmed until he was in his late 80s. He remained active until he had one leg amputated just below the knee as a result of a blood clot. He could still ride a horse even after he lost the leg. I helped him carve a peg leg from an ash timber after he lost his leg. I helped him up on his big horse, Trigger, for his last rides on horseback. It was one of my saddest times when he died on August 17, 1951, at age 90.

Grandpa and Grandma Tyson

Grandpa Tyson, Lemuel Cylas Tyson Jr., was born in Denton County, Texas in 1887, one of a large family of early settlers in

the area. Great Grandpa Tyson, Lemuel Cylas Tyson, Sr. was a skilled carpenter, blacksmith and a farmer. Grandpa learned his trades from his father. At age 19, Grandpa Tyson found work as a carpenter in Mangum, Oklahoma. There, he met a young lady named Sophia Lilly Snellen. She was from Indiana and happened to be visiting a sister who lived in Mangum at the time. They were married in Mangum in December 1906. Grandma never returned to Indiana, where her prosperous family lived.

Grandpa Tyson after retirement, about 1965.

Grandpa was a stout and busy man, with strict standards of morality and hard work. He built many of the early homes around Willow and Mangum. He raised his family on a series of farms around Willow. The children did the farm work while Grandpa brought home cash from his carpenter and blacksmith trades.

Grandpa established a general store in Willow. The store had good sales, but Grandpa was too generous with customer credit so the store failed. Grandpa returned to his carpenter trade and another rented farm. Nothing remains of Willow but a few old foundations of buildings.

In 1935, Grandpa Tyson followed the Booker family to Antlers. He settled on a 160 acre rented farm across the road east of Hall Corner. One of his main crops was sorghum, from which he made sorghum syrup. He used a horse-powered press to get the juice out of the cane, then he cooked the juice in a wood-fired furnace. His syrup was very strong, but good. He raised cash by selling the syrup in town.

Grandma Tyson as a young wife.

Grandma Tyson never seemed to be in good health. She never spent time with the grandchildren, so I never got to know her very well. I have very few memories of her.

Grandpa never had much of a sense of humor when the joke was on him. One rainy day, to avoid wading the mud and manure in the barnyard, he carried a bale of hay close behind some horses that were standing under a shed. One of them kicked the hay bale Grandpa was carrying, knocking him into the barnyard flat on his back. He was a stinking, soggy mess, and as mad as a wet hen, when he came to the house. He never did see the humor that everyone else saw in it.

All of Grandpa Tyson's children except Wayne, Fern and Leon

had married and moved away by the time World War II started. Elmer and Leon went away to war in Europe. In 1943, Grandpa moved to Mustang, Oklahoma so he could have greater access to carpentry work near Oklahoma City. Grandma Tyson died there on December 7, 1943. Grandpa built a store and several houses, which provided rental income for his later years.

Grandpa remained strong in body and mind as long as he lived. He was a fierce domino competitor who took great pleasure in beating any challenger. He died in December 1977 and was buried at the Mustang Cemetery.

Mom and Dad

Dad was 18 years old when the Booker family moved to Greer County in 1927. He and his brother drove a wagon loaded with canned fruit and vegetables to Greer County as part of the move. He had not finished high school and did not enroll in school in western Oklahoma. Although he did not finish school, he remained an avid reader all of his life. He worked at various farming and ranching jobs in Texas and Colorado while helping with Grandpa Booker's farm. He enrolled in a flight school in San Antonio, Texas in 1929, but ran out of money before he could achieve his pilot's license. He then tried to enlist in the Army Aviation Cadets, but was turned down because of a lung injury he had suffered as a young boy.

Mom was the fourth of nine children. Grandpa Tyson believed in having his children work hard on the farm. Mom had considerable responsibility in taking care of younger brothers and sisters as well. She was a good student and enjoyed school. She rode in a school wagon to and from school. I remember her talking about taking warm bricks in the wagon to keep her feet warm on cold winter days. She did not finish high school due to a need to work the family farm and later marriage to Dad.

Mom and Dad were married October 3, 1931 at Mangum. After they married, they lived in the basement of Grandpa Booker's farmhouse. Grandma Booker and Mom became very close. Grandma said Mom was like the daughter she never had.

The basement where the newlyweds lived was originally

a dugout used as a temporary shelter for cowboys who herded cattle along one of the old cattle trails from Texas to Kansas. Grandpa's house was built on top of the cowboy shelter, so that it became a basement for the house. I was born there on November 26, 1934.

Mom and Dad hired themselves out for picking cotton and any other work that could be found in the depressed economy of the time. They ran a small store and filling station somewhere in Greer County for about a year. In 1935, when I was about six months old, they drove their Durant coupe to Antlers as part of the move of the larger Booker and Tyson families.

The climate then was very hot, windy and dusty. There were very few farm ponds then, so water for cattle was scarce. Mom and Dad settled on a farm near Cloudy Tower in the Kiamichi Mountains northeast of Antlers. Cloudy Tower's climatic records show that it is the wettest spot in Oklahoma. Dad kept all of the Booker family cattle there because water was available even during the severe drought conditions prevailing then. Dad hunted for most of the meat we needed and Mom raised a good garden. We were reasonably self sufficient, even though the environment was quite crude.

Life at Hall Corner

The road intersection at the northeast corner of Grandpa's farm was known as Hall Corner. Dad and Mom moved our little family into a tiny two-room cabin at Hall Corner in 1938. My earliest memories are of life around Hall Corner. The cabin was only about 360 square feet in two rooms and was crammed with furniture and belongings for 3 people, later 5 people. Dad built a log barn, a chicken house and a smokehouse. He planted a large orchard and fenced a plot of land for Mom's vegetable garden.

Dad bought a 1937 Chevrolet truck, one of the few trucks in the area. He hired his truck out to haul cattle, corn or peanuts for area farmers. I often rode with him in the old truck all over southeast Oklahoma, sometimes as far away as the Oklahoma City stock yards.

Dad bought a peanut picker, baler and tractor just before World War II. During the summers, he and several hired hands baled hay. In the fall season, he used the peanut picker and baler rig to harvest peanut crops for farmers in the area. He set the thresher up in the middle of the field and powered it with a long belt from a belt drive on the tractor. Somebody would heave the peanut vines into the front end of the peanut picker with a pitchfork. The peanuts came trickling out the side while hay was thrown out the back. Some of the men sacked and stacked the peanuts while others baled the peanut hay. When they were finished, the field was bare sand. Hogs rooted out the few goobers left, so there was nothing left of the peanut crop in the field. This practice depleted the soil, leaving it exposed to erosion by wind and rain. Much of the land was badly eroded by the time I graduated from high school.

Mom and Dad after 50 years of marriage.

Dad was the best animal trainer in the community. He raised and trained a horse he called Smokey. Dad could plow the garden with Smokey without using a bridle or lines. Smokey would obey his commands precisely, plowing straight ahead until his breast touched the fence, then turning carefully so as to not step on any plants when Dad commanded "C'mere haw, Smokey." He could also ride him with no bridle, with Smokey obeying his voice commands.

By the time I was four years old, it was my job to go after the cows at evening milking time. Dad put me on Smokey's bare back and sent me after the cows. Smokey knew what to do, so I was just along for the ride. One afternoon, I fell off and somehow landed on my back between Smokey's front feet. Smokey was standing on my shirt tail so I couldn't get up. Smokey wouldn't move for fear of stepping on me. Dad heard my screams and came to investigate. He found Smokey quietly looking down at me but not moving. Dad calmly told Smokey to stand still while he picked Smokey's foot up so I could get out of there.

One day, a badly starved white pup with black speckles wandered up to our house. I got some food and water for her. By the time Dad got home that day, we were the best of friends. Dad could see that she was a purebred Llewellyn Setter, so he agreed we could keep her. I named her Porky. Dad trained her to hunt quail after we nursed her back to health. When Dad whistled a certain way, she would stop running and look at Dad for his command. A wave of his hand was enough to send her to a certain thicket he had in mind. Porky became widely respected as the best quail dog in the area.

People helped each other in the Hall community. When Dutch Coffman got sick, the neighbors brought their teams, cultivators and hoes to get his crops in shape until he could get back on his feet. Families helped each other on hog killing days. They traded labor for shaking and threshing peanuts. When neighbors came to help we could always count on good fried chicken, sweet potatoes and hot rolls. It seemed like those cooperative labor days were as much social meetings as anything.

Hall School had about 30 students when I started the first grade. The school had two teachers, one for the fifth through eight grades in the "big room" and one for the first through fourth grades in the "little room." The teachers often relied on the brighter students in the upper grades to help the younger ones with their lessons. On warm days the teachers would let us sit under the giant oak trees in the schoolyard to learn our spelling words with the help of an older student.

I started having eye trouble when I was in the second grade. My eyes itched and burned, so I rubbed them, making matters very much worse. Dad took me to several doctors about my eye trouble. A doctor in Hugo finally diagnosed my problem as "granulated eyelids." Every Thursday I walked two miles east to Dee Murray's store on the highway to catch a bus to Hugo for treatment. The doctor turned my eyelids inside out and scraped them with some sort of tool. It was painful. My condition showed no improvement so we discontinued treatment after a year.

The Hall schoolhouse served as a church on Sundays. Reverend Charley Martin, a local farmer, was the pastor for many years. He was not well educated, but he knew the Bible from cover to cover and could preach a powerful sermon. Church members loved him because of his selfless service and devotion to God.

Hall Church was an important part of community life. Most of our neighbors attended Sunday school and church. Some men brought their families but didn't go to church or Sunday school themselves. They stood around under the trees outside the schoolhouse, discussing their crops and other items of current interest while the women and children went to Sunday school and church. At least once per year, Hall Community had an "all day singing and dinner on the ground." The schoolyard was covered with cars, wagons, saddle horses and every kind of conveyance. They started early in the morning and sang church songs all day, with only a noon break for "dinner." Mom and Grandma Booker were always faithful in attendance at Sunday school and church. Grandpa never attended church. All of his boys grew up the same way. If Dad ever went to church, I never knew of it.

Airplanes

Dad enrolled in a flying school in San Antonio in 1929, but ran out of money before finishing. He tried to join the Army Aviation Cadets, but failed the physical examination because of a lung injury he suffered when he was nine years old. He took up flying again while we lived at Hall Corner. He took lessons from Jack Long, an Antlers banker, who operated two planes out of a grass landing strip two miles east of Hall Corner. However, he never took his check ride to get his license.

I was cutting weeds one day when I saw Jack Long's yellow

J3 Cub fly overhead. It went into a little dive then pulled up at a steep angle until it stalled. For a moment, it seemed to fall backwards, then flipped over and dove nearly straight down. As it pulled out of the dive, I could hear the wind whistling through the struts. As I watched the little yellow airplane drift out of sight to the west, playing as it went, I knew I would like to fly an airplane. My lifelong love affair with airplanes began that day.

One day, an Army Air Force C47 lost an engine and made a forced landing at Jack Long's airstrip. I was amazed by the size of it as it sat half bogged down in the soft soil. Large formations of military planes overhead were a common sight during the war. I couldn't think about my school work when a large formation of planes came over, with the awesome throbbing sound of so many big engines.

After the Antlers tornado in April 1945, Dad bought a ride for me in Jack Long's Aeronca. Jack flew me over Antlers to look over the damage. I was as much impressed with the feel and sound of the little aircraft as with the tornado damage. I knew for sure then that I wanted to learn to fly.

The Antlers Tornado

At about 4:30 PM on April 12, 1945, I arrived home from Hall School, where I was nearing the end of my fifth grade. Coincidentally, President Roosevelt had died just an hour earlier at Warm Springs, Georgia. After a while, Uncle Jack's truck stopped in front of the cabin to let Mom off. She had bought a few groceries at Antlers then caught a ride home with Jack.

Thunderstorms were moving in from the west. A few minutes after Mom arrived, I noticed a dark, swirling cloud southwest of us and pointed it out to Mom. She told me that it was a very bad tornado and it was coming toward us. Our little cabin was exposed on the top of a hill and there was no place for us to seek shelter. We saw Grandpa, Jack and Gladys running to Grandpa's cellar, just a quarter mile west, but there was no time for us to get there. Mom was seven months pregnant with Kaye, so she couldn't run anyway. We had little choice but to watch as the tornado approached. I understood that our lives could end in a few minutes, yet Mom made me feel calm about it. We watched out the front door as the tornado passed about ½ mile northwest of us and moved on toward Antlers.

After a while, neighbors in cars, trucks and wagons began moving past Hall Corner on the way to check on neighbors to the north and west. Mom made me stay at home. Before long, news came back to us that several of our neighbors had been killed or hurt and their houses were destroyed. The Jim Pilcher family was killed except for two young girls. Uncle Jack found the girls wandering around in the pasture, one of them badly wounded. Norma Jean Pilcher had been sitting at the desk in front of me less than an hour before she was killed. Just up the road from the Pilchers, the Engles were left lying on the floor, with the whole house gone from around them, but they were barely hurt. Their piano was still sitting on the floor where it had been before the storm.

The news from Antlers was very bad. Over half of the homes and businesses in the city were totally destroyed. There was nothing left standing in a quarter mile swath across the southeast half of town. There had been no warning and very few people had storm shelters. The Antlers American, published one week later, listed 68 dead and 343 injured. The final death toll was set at 84 killed.

Dad heard about the Antlers tornado while working at a construction site for a new ammunition plant at Camden, Arkansas. He caught a bus to Dee Murray's store, two miles east of our house and ran home as fast as he could to see if we had been hit. When he saw that we were OK, he caught a ride to town and volunteered for service. He worked the next three days in a temporary morgue.

The morning after the tornado, I walked to town. As I crossed Beaver Bridge on the south edge of town, I came into the path of destruction. Giant oak trees in the park were completely destroyed. Pieces of sheet iron, splintered lumber, clothes, and every kind of debris imaginable were scattered everywhere. I saw a dead mule stuck in the fork of a tree. Soldiers with rifles were patrolling the streets. Everybody seemed to be digging through the remains of houses. As I watched men removed some bodies from the wreckage of a building.

SEARCH FOR GREENER PASTURES

Oregon

A migration from Oklahoma to California and Oregon that began during the dust bowl days continued during World War II. There was much talk around Hall Community about good jobs in defense plants and big farms in California and Oregon. Dad was thinking of going west somewhere to take one of the good jobs available. He considered going to Alaska, even while the Japanese occupied the Aleutian islands of Kiska and Attu.

The time for action came in February 1944, when the Ben Herman family decided to move to Oregon. Mr. Herman had a large family, but his older boys had been drafted. None of his family living at home could drive a car. He hired Dad to transport his family to Oregon. Dad and Mr. Herman stretched a big tarpaulin over the sideboards of our old 1937 Chevrolet truck to make a shelter for the Herman family, a bed and some furniture on the back of the truck. There was a spirit of high adventure as the Herman family said their good-byes and crowded into the small space remaining on the truck. I watched the truck and its dust cloud disappear over the hill to the east, wishing I could go with them.

Dad's original plan was to deliver the Hermans to Oregon, look around for a few days, then return to Oklahoma. While looking around he met Charley Hart, who owned considerable farmland around Jefferson, Oregon. Dad sent a letter, saying he had a taken a job on Charley Hart's farm that included a good furnished house, so we should join him there. We packed a large steamer trunk and prepared for a train ride to Oregon.

We were excited and nervous as we stood in front of the Antlers Depot watching the train come into view from the south. None of us had ever been on a train or gone farther from home than Oklahoma City. Soon, our feelings of excitement and apprehension were calmed by the clicking of wheels on the rails and seeing farms and small towns glide silently by the window.

The next day, we were on a faster train out of Kansas City that didn't stop so often.

By the time we reached Salt Lake City, we were out of the food mom had brought aboard for us to live on. She decided to get off the train to restock our food supply during the layover at Salt Lake City. I fell asleep while she was gone, but woke up suddenly when I realized the train was moving again and Mom was not there. Fortunately, the car was only being moved to another track. After a while, Mom finally came aboard, looking hot and excited. She was terrified when she saw that the train was gone when she returned from shopping. It had taken her a while to find the train again and she was terrified that she would miss it. We stayed close together for the rest of the trip.

Our house in Oregon had lots of rooms on two floors. It was nicer than any house I had ever seen. I had a bedroom all to myself. The farm had large fields of beans, onions, flax, squash and peppermint. Most men had been drafted, so Mom joined other women who worked as field hands. It was very hard work so she was always exhausted when she came home. Dad worked at tilling the fields and providing for the field hands. I washed dishes and cleaned the house as I stayed home to take care of Sue and Les.

I liked our life in Oregon. Everything was different from what I was accustomed to, but I was happy there. My eye problems were gone. Mom liked Oregon and she wanted us to stay there. However, Dad was always drawn like a magnet to Antlers. After we had been in Oregon about three months, Dad ran the front wheels of the truck up on some blocks in the front yard and started to take the engine apart. Mom told me tearfully that he was getting the truck ready to return to Hall Corner.

Back to Hall

Hall held little cheer for the returning Booker family. The little two-room cabin seemed much smaller than it was before we lived in the big house in Oregon. My eye problems returned. World War II was a worry on the mind of everybody. All the young men from the community had gone away to fight a war. The news was not good from some of them. Those left at home struggled to make a crop and sustain themselves. Everything was rationed, so we had to make do mostly on food raised on the farm. Dad resumed his trucking business, but gasoline and tires were rationed, so he had trouble keeping the truck in operation. He finally moved to a job on a new ammunition plant that was being built at Camden, Arkansas.

While Dad was gone, Mom and I learned to survive alone on Hall Corner. We had no car, but Mom couldn't drive anyway. I borrowed a horse from Grandpa Booker and rode bareback to Antlers for groceries. The orchard and garden that Dad had established a few years earlier provided most of our food. I milked two cows and fed a couple of hogs that became food for our table.

There was no electricity at Hall, so there were no electric lights or fans. Mom's small wood-burning cook stove made our tiny kitchen unbearably hot when she cooked on summer days. Kaye was born June 6, 1945. That made a family of six living in a little two-room cabin of about 360 square feet. I again joined the dwindling number of students at Hall School. There was little organized teaching. Much of our study was outside under a tree with an older student presiding. Most of that time in Hall School was wasted.

There was lots of excitement when news came over the radio that Germany, then Japan had surrendered. The returning soldiers had much to tell about their experiences in the war. Doyle Barnes, Dad's childhood friend after whom I was named, told of riding in gliders and crash-landing into hedgerows behind German lines. Leon Tyson talked about being a military policeman. Elmer Tyson told of fighting house to house through France. Guy Emery told how his B24 Liberator was shot up badly twice, forcing him to ditch his plane both times in the South Pacific.

Idaho

In the winter of 1945-46, Dad again decided to try his luck out west. He departed for Oregon with an intention of eventually getting to Alaska. After working at various jobs in Oregon, he found a job on a dairy farm near Buhl, Idaho. Late that spring, he sent word that our family should again take a train west to join him.

The dairy farm was owned by a German immigrant named Karsten Jess, who had fought in the American Army in the war against the Germans. It was a prosperous farm with a good herd of Holstein cows. The pastures and fields were irrigated with an elaborate trench irrigation system. The dairy barn had automatic milkers and a central milk collection system. Even though this was a prosperous farming community, Dad was not happy there. It was soon time to move on again.

By late summer of 1946, Dad was ready to attempt the move to Alaska that he had so long dreamed of. He bought a 1934 Chevrolet sedan and a small home-built trailer. We loaded what we owned into the trailer and left the dairy farm enroute to Seattle. Dad's plan was that Mom and the children would live in Seattle while he would continue to Alaska. He would send for the family after finding a job and a place for us to live.

As we passed through Lewiston, Idaho, Dad ran into a farmer named Bill Heinrich, who was looking for help to harvest his wheat crop. Mr. Heinrich owned a large wheat farm and cattle ranch near Genesee, Idaho. He offered Dad a job plus a nicely furnished two-story house. Dad decided to take the job to build up a cash reserve before continuing to Alaska.

I joined the seventh grade at Genesee School. There were five times as many students in the seventh grade as Hall had in the whole school at its peak attendance. Every seventh grade student played in the band or sang in the choir. I was hopelessly behind in the subjects taught in the seventh grade, so my grades were poor. However, after a period of adjustment, I became more at ease in my new environment and was happy there.

The Heinrich ranch barn still had the stalls and harnesses used by the 20-horse teams that had drawn the large gangplows and combines before tractors came to the farm. Stored in the attic of the shop building, we found a toboggan, a snow sled and several pairs of homemade skis. The farm was very hilly and there was plenty of snow, so it was a good place to play with those new toys. The house was a luxury for us. It had more than enough rooms for us to have individual bedrooms. It had a furnished formal dining and living room, electric lights and a wall-mounted "tail-twister" telephone. Mom had a water pump with a sink in the kitchen.

Mom liked Idaho even better than she had liked Oregon. She enjoyed her new friends, especially the Sweeneys, our nearest neighbors. She liked the vigorous, friendly, hard working nature of the people there. Janice joined the family early on the morning of May 29, 1947, at the Heinrich ranch.

I came home from school one day shortly after starting the eighth grade at Genesee to learn that we would start packing for the trip back to Antlers and Hall Corner. Mom was very unhappy about it. Only many years later would I know how much she disliked life at Hall and how she tried to have us moved from there permanently.

In October 1947, we loaded the old 1934 Chevrolet and the little wooden-box trailer for the long trip back to Antlers. With two adults, five children and all of our possessions, the old Chevrolet was very cramped and badly overloaded. Its radiator boiled on every substantial grade. My job was to keep several gallons of water ready and refill the radiator when it boiled. The trailer was overloaded, so it broke down several times. We arrived at Hall after 10 miserable days on the road.

Hall again

With a family of seven, the little two-room cabin at Hall corner was out of the question. Dad rented an 80 acre farm a half mile north of Hall corner, which we called the Spears place. The house was a quarter mile off the road down a frequently impassable lane and beside a swamp. The house was about 50 years old and in very bad condition. A fireplace was the only source of heat and it consumed enormous amounts of wood. It was my job to cut and haul the wood.

Our previously reliable old Chevrolet began falling apart. First the left rear door fell off while Dad was driving and was damaged beyond redemption. After that, we had the only three door Chevy in the county. The reverse and low gears went out so we had to start off in second gear and be careful not to get caught needing reverse. The clutch failed somehow, so that as I learned to drive it, I had to take my left shoe off so I could pull the clutch out with my toes.

Even though an Antlers School bus came past our house, Dad had Sue and me rejoin the nearly extinct Hall school. We had six students scattered over eight grades in one room. That was the final year of Hall School. I learned very little that year.

Near the end of my eighth grade year, Dad bought a small, untrained mule named Joe and told me to make a work mule out of him. Joe was mean and would bite or kick at the slightest opportunity. One day, I hitched Joe to a one-row planter to plant watermelons. He promptly ran away with the planter. After I caught him again, I loaded the sled with sand and hitched Joe to it. He tried to run away again but he couldn't pull the load very fast. I jumped on the sled and whipped his rump with all of the pent up frustration within me. When he stopped trying to run, I whipped him until he ran some more. After we were both exhausted, I hitched him to the planter and planted the watermelons. There were many more such incidents with Joe before I persuaded Dad to send him back to the sale barn.

During the winter of 1948-49, Dad and our neighbor, Nudge VanSickle, began trapping mink to earn a few extra dollars. They used rabbit parts as bait for the traps. One rabbit that Dad shot appeared to be sick. Before long, Dad became seriously ill with tularemia, or rabbit fever. His recovery was very slow and costly. We were deep in debt even before the medical bills arrived. It was decided that I would make the 1949 crop while Dad worked away from home to try to reduce our debts. He was still sick that summer and his construction work income barely covered his expenses.

I was 14 years old and knew almost nothing about raising a crop or driving a team. With Dad away, I was totally on my own resources. The tractor that Dad had used for farming the previous year was gone. I would have to try to make my first crop with horse-drawn tools. A few of Mr. Spears' old horse drawn implements were scattered around the farm but were in very poor condition. I replaced the rotted wooden parts and built up a passable set of horse-drawn farming tools.

Grandpa Booker said I could use his big buckskin colt, named Trigger, as a plow horse, but I would have to break him to work. Dad bought an old logging mule named Ike at the sale barn in Antlers. Having never worked a team before, I would have to train Grandpa's unbroken colt and an old logging mule to work as a team. I was far from ready, but the calendar said it was time to start preparing a seedbed.

I decided to prepare a seedbed with a lister, a plow that throws dirt to the left and right to make a deep furrow. I started trying to break my odd team to pull implements while also trying to learn to use a lister. My lister furrows on the first few acres were crooked and the spacing varied widely. Uncle Pete came by one day laughed and shook his head at the sight. By the time he dropped by again, I was finishing the first 30 acres. By that time, the team and I had gotten our act together. My furrows were straight and evenly spaced. Uncle Pete looked pleased and said he thought I might be OK after all. I finished planting about the time my class at Antlers High was finishing the ninth grade. I had missed most of the critical final weeks of that year, so my grades were very poor.

I got a good stand of watermelons, peanuts and corn, but the crab grass followed quickly. I had to learn to use a walking cultivator while making the team and the cultivator wheels stay on top of the lister ridges. I soon realized that planting in lister furrows was a bad idea. As the summer progressed, I achieved a sort of equilibrium with my conditions and I began to take some pride in the progress of my crop. My peanuts, with their deep roots, survived a long dry spell better than any peanut crop in the neighborhood so my lister furrows paid off after all.

Grandpa Booker recommended that I stack my peanuts in shocks for curing at harvest time, rather than windrow them as almost all farmers did. It was really hard work, but I hired a few of my neighborhood friends to help dig and shock the peanuts. My shocked peanuts survived a long, dreary rainy spell after harvest while my neighbors' windrowed peanuts were mostly ruined. We had about $400 left after selling the peanuts and paying the bills. My crop brought in enough to pay off our debts in town and open up our credit again.

Later that fall, Uncle Arthur decided to return his family from Oklahoma City to Antlers. Uncle Jack agreed to move the family in his big International truck and asked me to go along and help load furniture. We left Antlers about 3 AM. We finished loading Jack's truck and Arthur's old 1938 Chevrolet panel truck about mid afternoon. Jack and Arthur had started nipping at a whiskey bottle in the morning. Jack seemed OK but Arthur was not fit to drive as we loaded everybody into the two vehicles and started the long drive to Antlers.

I rode with my cousins, Bill, Jerry and Orland in Arthur's panel truck. A sudden traffic situation developed on South Shields Avenue. Uncle Arthur overreacted and put the panel truck into a skid that resulted in rolling it upside down. I found myself lying on the pavement in the middle of the road, unhurt except for some scrapes and bruises. The panel truck had come to rest on its top. As I ran toward it, I could hear Orland yelling for Bill and Jerry to get the washing machine off of him. Two chicken coops had broken open and startled chickens were scattering everywhere. Most of the fruit jars in the back of the panel truck had broken so canned peaches were oozing over everything in the truck. The battery, which was mounted under the passenger side floorboard, had spilled acid on Bill and me.

After a wrecker set the panel truck upright, Jack poured oil in it and found that it would still run. After the highway patrolman departed, Jack announced that he would drive the panel truck and I would drive his truck to Antlers. Arthur was not in shape to drive anything. Ruth argued that I was too young and both Jack and Arthur were too drunk to drive, but she lost the argument. I was 14 years old and had only driven a truck a few times to pick up watermelons in the fields. I did have experience driving our old Chevrolet car, but never on a highway.

Aunt Ruth, Gwen and Orland crowded into the cab with me. Bill and Jerry rode on top of the load and covered themselves with a tarpaulin to provide some protection from the cold wind. Jack told me to follow behind him and keep the panel truck in sight. However, he drove too fast and we lost sight of the panel truck.

I knew the way to Antlers, so we continued.

After dark, fog began forming in the low places. As I drove into a fog bank, I suddenly saw a white horse in my lane, almost invisible in the fog. I swerved the truck hard left and came close to a deep ditch on the left before I regained control. If I had gone a little more to the left, we would surely have rolled over, killing at least Bill and Jerry and possibly all of us. We had escaped death by inches for the second time that day. I was so shaken that I could barely drive. I stopped the truck at the first opportunity.

Aunt Ruth was trying to calm me down when Jack and Arthur drove up from behind in the badly bent panel truck. They were in a happy mood. It turned out that they had stopped for another bottle of whisky.

An Antlers High School senior.

By the time we got to Antlers, the battery acid that had spilled on me during the wreck was eating away at my clothes. I was skinned and bruised and I had been awake almost 24 hours. Mom and Dad looked dumbstruck as I told them what had happened the next morning.

By the end of 1949, Mom had quite enough of our situation. We had experienced one tragedy and hardship after another since returning to Hall Community. The old Spears house was falling down around us. The old Chevrolet had died. It was time for a new start and Mom made that clear to Dad.

Near the end of the year, Dad came home one day to say he had made a deal to rent the Veal farm, an 80 acre farm about three miles west from Hall Corner. The Veal place had a reasonably sound four-room house and a big barn, electricity, and some rich new ground in the bottom below the house. Dad bought a well-matched team of horses and a good wagon as we moved to the Veal place. He bought a war-surplus US Army ambulance, which served as a truck and rudimentary transportation for the family.

I made a crop again at the Veal place the summer following my high school sophomore year but the crop was not critical to the family welfare as it had been the previous year. By that time, Dad was well again and had started following pipeline construction work, which he would do until retirement. Dad's income from the pipeline jobs could sustain us, so the crop was only a supplement to family income.

While Dad was gone, I traded the old ambulance, which needed repairs, for a 1928 Model A Ford in top condition. It was the first time the family had reliable transportation since returning to Oklahoma. With the Model A available, I got a job at Barden Taylor's Grocery and Feed Store in Antlers. The grocery store was my first job that involved mixing with people, and I enjoyed it. I began to build some self confidence.

Hall School had done little to prepare me for high school. I was a poor reader and was far behind in math and English. I missed most of the last two months of my freshman year to get my crop started. I barely squeaked by some of my courses. I missed much of the fall of my sophomore year to harvest the crop. I missed some of the final weeks to put in another crop. I failed algebra and did not do well in other courses except agriculture, where I always did well. Three teachers came to my aid.

Dr. Carl Skinner retired and bought a farm in the Hall Community while I was in the eighth grade. He pushed me to become a public speaker, insisting that I compete in the public speaking contests in the Future Farmers of America (FFA). He helped me write speeches and worked with me on my delivery. Because of his backing, I won a few public speaking contests. Dr. Skinner made going to college sound reasonable, possible and expected. He taught me to raise my sights and to try for things I would never have attempted.

Mr. Bill Simms was a young agriculture teacher when I entered my freshman year at Antlers High School. He had large classes, so he did not notice me at first. As we got better acquainted, he recognized that I could not afford a calf or pig for a project, which was required of every boy in the FFA, but he helped me to participate in horticulture and public speaking contests. He gave me jobs I felt were important at the FFA rodeo. Because of his interest, I always did well in agriculture classes. He seemed to take a special interest in me and he encouraged me to go to college.

Mrs. Pearl Farr was a strict and dedicated English teacher at Antlers High School. She insisted that English was the most important course we would take in high school, and that what we learned in her class would determine how well we would do in life. I paid careful attention in her classes. She would stop what she was doing to give me a little extra help when I struggled. Because of her, I progressed from almost total ignorance of English grammar to a fair competence during that freshman year. No other English teacher in high school or college would teach me as much about English as Mrs. Farr did. Later, Governor Bellmon appointed her to his School Textbook Advisory Board. No teacher could be more deserving of the honor.

As I neared graduation, I was not sure what I wanted to do, but I was sure I wanted to move away from Antlers. I borrowed $25, bought a suitcase, a few clothes and a bus ticket to Carrolton, Ohio, where Dad was working on a pipeline job. The next morning after graduation, I saw tears in my Mother's eyes as I said goodbye and boarded the bus. We both knew I was leaving Antlers and Hall Community permanently.

SECOND QUARTER - EDUCATION

OKLAHOMA A&M COLLEGE

Decisions

When I graduated from high school, I was inclined to try to go to college, mainly because of the urging of Dr. Carl Skinner and Mr. Bill Simms. However, it was by no means a firm decision. One day during that first pipeline construction season, I noticed a man with clean dress pants standing on the pipe and working what I later learned was a slide rule. He told me that he was an engineer for the pipeline company. He told me a little about what he did, and I was very interested. I began thinking about being an engineer. Before that, I had thought that, if I went to college at all, I would probably study animal science because I liked ranching much better than peanut farming.

I caught a bus to Stillwater to begin my college career in August 1952. I stumbled through the enrollment process until I found myself sitting in front of a kind lady who asked me what I intended to major in. I answered "engineering." She looked patiently at me and asked, "what kind of engineering?" I was stumped. It had never crossed my mind that there would be more than one kind of engineering. After what seemed to me like a long period of thinking, I answered "Well, sort of - - - general engineering, I guess." She looked at me for a few seconds, then entered something on her form. I later learned that I had enrolled myself in the School of General Engineering. Later that year, I changed my major to mechanical engineering, aeronautical engineering option. All freshman and sophomore men were required to take basic ROTC. I didn't hesitate a second to enroll in Air Force ROTC because of my fascination with airplanes.

A gentleman, whose job it was to help me get enrolled in the right classes, noticed that I had flunked algebra, and only made a D the second time I took it, and that I had no geometry or trigonometry. He told me that I would have to take a five-credit algebra class and a three-credit geometry class before I would be allowed to take engineering courses or other math courses.

These courses were remedial in nature, and would not count toward graduation. By the standards used for admission today, I would not have been admitted at all.

I became discouraged, as freshmen frequently do, during my first semester. Classes were difficult and I had trouble finding time to study after working two jobs. I began to have serious doubts about my aptitude for college. Three older boys occupied the room next to my tiny room in a boarding house. One was Charlie Smith, a junior from Canadian, Oklahoma. I was in awe of Charlie. He took an interest in me, so I mentioned the remedial math and the other indications that I was not cut out to be an engineer and maybe not college material at all.

An Oklahoma A&M College sophomore.

Charlie was always positive in his convictions. He declared that I was a "diamond in the rough," and that I just needed a little polishing. He immediately took me to the Baptist Student Union (BSU) and began introducing me around like I was a friend he had known all his life. From that day on, Charlie made sure I attended every activity of the BSU. He also towed me to the First Baptist Church of Stillwater. It was the first church I had ever been inside besides the Hall Freewill Baptist Church. Charlie continued to take a personal interest in me that entire freshman year. His influence had much to do with my not growing so discouraged that I gave up college. During the next year, Charlie continued to try to smooth off the rough edges in me and to encourage me to be more outgoing. He said I was a very introverted and complex individual, and that I was a challenge for him.

Earlene

One day in March 1953, as I was about to cross the street near Bennett Hall, a couple of girls raced by on bicycles. One of them waved and greeted me with "Hi Ray!" I finally realized that she was Earlene Hobbs. whom I had met her during a BSU visit to an old folks' home. I called to ask if she would consider being my date to a BSU picnic at Lake Carl Blackwell. I had not had a date with any girl before joining the BSU. I had a few dates with a couple of other girls before I met Earlene. Something seemed to click with her, and I found myself thinking about her much of the time. We began dating steadily during the next year. We were both regulars in our attendance of BSU activities, so we began going to those activities together. We soon expanded our outings to a few athletic events and movies to the extent our schedules could stand it.

We were beginning to be very serious about each other in our junior year. We moved to the stage of visiting our parents

Our wedding picture with Earl and Martha Hobbs and
Mom. Dad was unable to attend.

together. Earlene's parents lived on a farm on the Arkansas River bottom a few miles downstream from Cleveland, a farm that later was covered by Lake Keystone. Earl and Martha

Hobbs were teachers at Cleveland High School. Her little brother, Lowell, was a student there, and was active in everything, as Earlene had been. Martha was very kind, but Earl kept testing me, and I got the feeling he wasn't very proud of what Earlene had dragged home. Earlene then visited my home at Antlers. It was quite different from the prosperous and goal-oriented environment she had come from. Yet, she was as gracious as she could be, and she thoroughly impressed my family.

We became engaged that fall. I knew little about buying a ring, so I just picked out one with the biggest stone I could buy with the money I had. We were married at Earlene's home church in Cleveland on March 18, 1955. It was a beautiful wedding with all of our extended families and many of our OSU friends in attendance. After a one weekend honeymoon, we were back in school.

Karen was due one year to the day after our wedding. Earlene became very sick as soon as she discovered she was pregnant. She stayed in our tiny apartment while I went away to work for the summer. When I learned how sick she was, I returned to Stillwater. The summer was hot and we had only one small fan, so the temperature in the little apartment was nearly unbearable. Fudgesicles were the only food she could eat without losing it immediately. I missed a mid-term exam that coincided with Karen's arrival. The loss of the mid-term grade really hurt my grade point average. I soon learned that working, studying and taking care of a little baby was quite a load.

Earlene resumed her studies during my fifth and final year and we graduated together in May 1957. She was magnificent in her ability to be a mother, wife and student at the same time.

Engineering Student

Mr. Raymond Caskey taught my remedial geometry class. He said he couldn't understand how someone could get out of high school with as little math as I had. He said that engineering is very math intensive, so I needed to work hard to catch up. He was a kind man and spent extra time with me. Because of him, I did fairly well in geometry. However, I had the first of a series of very poor math teachers for algebra. Trigonometry, calculus I and II and differential equations followed in order and were all struggles for me.

Dr. L. J. Fila taught aerodynamics, a subject I really wanted to do well in, but it was math-intensive and I was finding it difficult. Dr. Fila took an interest in me, helped me where I struggled, gave me advice and encouraged me to keep on trying. His influence was as vital as that of Dr. Carl Skinner, Mr. Bill Simms and Mrs. Pearl Farr in high school and played a major role in my ultimately becoming an engineer.

My savings from summer construction jobs were not sufficient for all expenses, so I always had one or two part time jobs. Stillwater was a small town and it was a competitive job market. I found a job sweeping the library, beginning at 4 AM and a second job at Marvin's Grocery, where I could earn $0.75 per hour. I held both jobs during most of my freshman year and similar jobs during later years. Study time was squeezed into the late night and breaks between classes and usually not very productive.

Dad gave me a $20 bill for Christmas of my junior year. That was the only assistance I received from anyone during my college career.

I worked at pipeline construction jobs at several locations around the US to pay for college expenses. Most of the time, I was hired as a common laborer, but was able at times to land jobs driving trucks or heavy construction equipment. It was hot, heavy work but it added to my motivation to finish college.

Even with my best efforts, I could not cover the expenses of college, especially after Earlene and I married. I was forced to apply for student loans from the Lew Wentz Foundation. I repaid the loans fully after graduation.

Reserve Officers Training Corps (ROTC)

Basic ROTC courses were required for all freshman and sophomore students. I was accepted in the Air Force ROTC. I was proud to wear the blue ROTC uniform for ROTC class and drill. I liked the discipline and order of military drill. I was selected to train with the AFROTC Leadership School. It was designed to teach leadership skills to a small squadron of cadets. Leadership training was above and beyond other ROTC duties and no extra credit was given for it. I was selected to command the Leadership School in my junior year.

I applied for and was accepted for advanced ROTC, leading to a commission in the US Air Force. I wanted very much to be an Air Force officer. The $26 per month we received for advanced ROTC was vital to our financial survival after Earlene and I were married.

I was ordered to attend ROTC summer camp at March Air Force Base, Riverside, California. We were given rides in Air Force planes and trained on military maneuvers. It was like a boot camp, with pre-dawn formations, marching, physical conditioning and inspections. We were given demerits for even minor flaws or failures. I managed to get through summer camp with a good record and minimal demerits, but was rated only average in leadership skills.

For the fall semester, I was selected as a squadron commander and was promoted to group commander for my final semester. I attained the rank of cadet Lt. Col. I was surprised to find myself one of the highest-ranking ROTC cadet officers. I still did not view myself a leader.

The big payoff for my efforts in ROTC came in my final semester when, for the first time, flight training was made available to those cadets that had been selected for active duty pilot training. Oklahoma A&M bought four new Piper Super Cubs for the flight training program. Those of us who were pilot training cadets were given a ground school, 35 hours of pilot training and a FAA check ride with no cost to the cadets.

My flight instructor was Lowell Hyfil, a World War II veteran, who had little patience and seemed to always be yelling in my ear. After about 8 hours of training, Lowell asked me to stop on the taxiway and he stepped out, leaving me alone in the aircraft. It was to be my first solo flight. I was suddenly scared and felt terribly alone in the aircraft, but the flight went well. I think I was about average as a student pilot, but I passed the check ride and was awarded a private pilot's license in March 1957. I was sure I was on my way to being an Air Force fighter pilot.

Career Path Choice

As graduation approached, Earlene and I had a big decision to make. I would soon be commissioned as a second lieutenant in the US Air Force. Since I had been selected for flight training and agreed to sign a three year contract with the Air Force, I could expect to spend two years in training and another year on active flying duty. I knew that at the end of that enlistment, I would have to make a choice about getting out of the service to take up my career as an aeronautical engineer or try to stay for a 20-year career in the Air Force. I wanted to have some basis for comparison before making that choice. I asked for and was granted a one-year delay of service so that I could take an engineering job for a year before going on active duty. We felt that would let us see both sides before we came to the major career decision.

ENGINEERING AT CHANCE VOUGHT

I interviewed with several of the big aircraft companies that made recruiting trips to the A&M campus. I was one of the few aeronautical engineering graduates who had not been able to do some summer work in the aeronautical engineering field. My construction jobs had not prepared me for competing in the aeronautical engineering job market. My school record was only average. I was fortunate that there were enough jobs available for the average graduates. I received offers from Douglas Aircraft in Tulsa, Northrop Aircraft at Cape Canaveral and Chance Vought Aircraft in Grand Prairie, Texas. I selected the Chance Vought job because it was located close to home and the work sounded interesting.

Earlene and I drove to Dallas with our little daughter, Karen, through rain and many detours due to washed out roads and bridges. That happened to be a week of record rains and floods in southern Oklahoma and north Texas.

We found a duplex in west Dallas, only about a twenty-minute drive from the Chance Vought Aircraft plant. We had very little furniture, so we bought what we thought we needed on credit. We soon found that my $4,800 salary barely covered the payments on our two-year-old Plymouth, the furniture and repayment of our Lew Wentz Foundation student loan. After a period of barely getting by, Earlene found a job as a secretary at Chance Vought.

Chance Vought employed 17,000 people in a huge plant in Grand Prairie, Texas. I worked in an enormous room on the second floor with hundreds of other engineers and draftsmen. I was a performance engineer on the Regulus II, a jet powered supersonic missile. The Regulus II had a powerful jet engine, tiny wings and was capable of Mach II speed. It was designed to be launched from submarines. My job was to compute performance data for flight tests and simulated missions. I spent all day every day working the long equations of motion for the aircraft in small increments of time from a rocket-assisted launch through the climb, cruise and terminal dive to the target. Some missions included test flights of a special version of the missile that had a landing gear and was designed to be recoverable.

I solved the equations of motion by use of huge spreadsheets and a sliderule, solving one step of the equation, then moving to the next, and so on. Any laptop computer today could do in a few milliseconds what took me a day or two. But, the work was extremely repetitive and soon became boring. I only saw the aircraft that I was computing performance data for as I walked past them on the assembly line enroute to the parking lot after work.

I was becoming disillusioned about the career I had chosen. I did not want to spend a career doing paper engineering. Engineers who had been at other companies led me to believe the life of an aeronautical engineer would be about the same at any company. I had become an aeronautical engineer because I liked airplanes, but my job had little or nothing to do with real airplanes.

I was restless for something more interesting to do, particularly if it had to do with airplanes. I spent considerable time hanging around airports in the area, talking to pilots and airplane owners. I got a few chances to fly with pilots who owned small planes. Those were interesting planes, but I could not see a way to connect my education with them. I began to think more seriously about the Air Force career that was still available to me. Chance Vought was convincing me that I would probably like the Air Force better.

A new Air Force officer.

As it turned out, a major career path choice had just been made. During the one year delay, the Air Force increased the contract obligations for beginning pilots from three to five years. I could keep my three commitment by choosing a non-flying job. I had been promised a great job at studying the performance of Russian fighters at Wright Patterson AFB if I would apply for it. I elected to not sign up for the five year commitment and apply for the WPAFB job. Much to my amazement, my orders were to report to The Pennsylvania State University for meteorology training. I was looking at a potentially completely new career choice.

A STUDENT AGAIN

Thirty-two of the new officers were assigned to The Pennsylvania State University. The pay for a Second Lieutenant was $272 plus a $70 housing allowance. We still had the same payments, but a much smaller paycheck. Most of the young officers had wives and small children, so we had plenty of companions to share our economic troubles with. That period of fellowship with the other officer-students and their wives was a good time in our young married life.

Fortunately for me, the summer was dedicated to a review of math and an introduction to meteorology. Most of the officer-students didn't need the math review, but it was vital for me. I dove into the study with a much greater dedication than ever before. For the first time, I was a full time student with no part time jobs. I began to comprehend most of what I had missed as I struggled through the Oklahoma A&M math classes.

The introductory course for meteorology was a hit with me. I liked the course, my professor and the students I studied with. Larry Davis, Jerry Bird, Dave Reeves and I developed the habit of studying together. Larry and Jerry had done well in their original undergraduate courses in electrical engineering and chemical engineering. Dave had been selected for meteorology, even though his undergraduate degree had been physical education, and his math background was worse than mine. Larry, Jerry and I pulled Dave along.

Dave had been trained as a coach in several sports, including tennis. I had never played tennis. The others were not very good, so Dave coached us in tennis. The four of us played at least once per week during the warm seasons. After some of Dave's coaching, I finally could hold my own with our foursome.

We began to notice that many of the Air Force wives were getting pregnant. There was a rumor that it had something to do with the State College water. Earlene and I discussed it, and decided it was time for us to have a second child. A doctor soon confirmed that Earlene was pregnant.

I walked a mile down a railroad track to the campus and back two or three times every day. The walks gave me time to think about things. I knew by then that I liked meteorology. I was beginning to believe a career in meteorology would be more interesting than my sliderule jockey job in aeronautical engineering. My professors said that a master's degree is necessary to advance in meteorology, and a PhD is required to teach meteorology. I began to think about getting an MS degree. I didn't even dream about a PhD.

I mentioned the idea of getting an MS degree in meteorology to Larry Davis. We began thinking about asking Penn State to give us graduate credit for our course work at Penn State The Dean of the Graduate School told me my Oklahoma A&M grades did not qualify me for graduate school, especially, he said, since Penn State was a tougher school than Oklahoma A&M. As I was about to leave, I asked if he had looked at my Penn State grades. He picked up my record and looked puzzled. I had nearly straight As at his school with the "higher standards." He then decided that he would admit me on the condition that I continue that level of achievement at Penn State. As a result, I was awarded 16 credits toward an MS degree for my Air Force courses at Penn State. I had no idea how I would ever be able to get back to Penn State to finish the MS degree.

As I was finishing my work at Penn State, I received a promotion to first lieutenant and orders to report for duty at Tinker Air Force Base, Midwest City, Oklahoma. The other members of my Air Force class were ordered to other bases around the world. We would not see many of them again.

A WORKING METEOROLOGIST

Tinker AFB

I reported for duty at Tinker AFB in August 1959. The detachment commander looked surprised when I walked into his office and gave a snappy salute, the way we were taught in ROTC leadership school. He looked puzzled as he sort of returned my salute. I wondered if I was supposed to walk in and say, "Hi, I'm Ray Booker."

I was assigned to work with two master sergeants for my

on-the-job training. Sgt. Dale Hall and his twin brother, Don, were enlisted forecasters who had earned their stripes the hard way. It was immediately obvious that all of my fancy college training didn't cut any mustard with them. The proof of a real forecaster was in how well he could forecast.

The Hall twins and Sergeant Gene Collett, started betting a quarter with me on the forecast of some meteorological variable, such as the maximum temperature for the day at Tinker or the lowest ceiling at Austin. I could see that my honor was at stake, so I participated in the game fully. I lost most of the time. Gene Collett was the one who really cleaned my plow. He had spent 14 years at Tinker by that time and knew every trick in the book. I eventually developed some skill in forecasting and earned the respect of the sergeants and my commander.

My job was to forecast weather for aircrews and for base operations. All forecasters worked rotating shifts. We plotted and analyzed our own maps and soundings because there was only limited guidance available from the Air Force Weather Center. It was up to us to develop a custom forecast for each user. Producing an accurate forecast was a great mental challenge that I enjoyed very much. We would know within a few hours how well the forecast verified and we could review our reasoning to sharpen our skills for next time. I became a moderately good forecaster and felt that I was contributing something important.

Lt. Booker, Tinker AFB weather forecaster.

I received a letter from the Air Force in October 1959 announcing a reduction in force that included officers in my category. I was given a choice of getting out of the Air Force in March or take an overseas assignment for an indefinite period of time. Earlene and I decided to take the option of getting out the next March. For my eight months of active duty, I received 13 months of meteorology education and 16 graduate credits. I considered myself very lucky.

Twins

Earlene was about as pregnant as a girl can get. She had been very sick for several months during the second pregnancy. She had become very skinny, just as she had with Karen. Her tummy looked like she had swallowed a watermelon seed.

On the last day of my Air Force career, our doctor examined Earlene. He told her she should proceed immediately to the hospital. I drove her to Mercy Hospital in Oklahoma City and waited in the hall as the admitting nurse examined her. I heard the nurse ask Earlene "Why didn't you tell us when you called that you are a multiple birth patient?" I stopped my pacing. I couldn't believe what I had just heard. I heard Earlene

Karen, Larry and Garry, just home from the hospital.

ask what she meant, then the nurse answer "Well, there are at least two in there, honey." The doctor had never hinted that she could be carrying twins. We were not smart enough to guess there were two babies from the size of her tummy.

Within a few minutes, and with a separation of only eight minutes, we were presented with twin boys. I was a basket case when I was finally allowed to walk into Earlene's room and saw her with two babies in her arms. She was already accustomed to the situation.

I enjoyed telling both of our parents about the surprise, and we had fun naming the boys. But the fun ended when we brought them home. Having two babies plus an active four year-old was a challenge of a lifetime. The twins never seemed to wake

41

up at the same time. It seemed that one or the other was demanding attention all the time. The boys came on my last day in the Air Force, so they cost only $5 each. If they had come the next day, they would have cost $250 each - much more money than we had available.

Career Decision Time

As the end of my Air Force service approached, it was time to choose between two potential careers. A flying career seemed out of the question since I had closed the Air Force career option. I had about equal education and practical experience in aeronautical engineering and meteorology. I did not want to return to being a sliderule jockey in some large defense plant. Yet, I had not discovered a way to make a living as a civilian meteorologist.

Harry Volkman, a popular TV meteorologist, left KWTV Channel 9 in Oklahoma City, for a major station in Chicago at about that time. Al Worth moved up to Harry's job, leaving a vacant second meteorologist job. I mentioned to Gene Collett one day that I had thought about trying for the TV meteorologist job, but I figured it was probably a waste of time. Gene said he thought I was well suited for the job, so he encouraged me to go for it.

There were only about twenty television meteorologists in the US then. Four of them were in Oklahoma City. Oklahomans had a very strong interest in weather, so TV meteorologists were viewed with great interest. Weather shows were the most important segment in determining TV newscast ratings. I had considerable trouble imagining myself in such a high profile position. Earlene kept telling me that I could do it. Finally, I worked up the courage to call the TV station and ask about the job. I was given an appointment for an interview.

I had not the slightest idea how to be a television meteorologist as I walked into the TV station for what I thought would be an interview. Al Worth and Edgar Bell, the station manager, immediately hustled me into a studio for an audition. Al asked me to take a few minutes to review the current Teletype data and fax charts, draw a map on the weather set, then present a weather program as though I was on the air. I hadn't thought about having to do anything like that. I tried to keep from shaking as I drew the fronts and isobars. I felt very awkward as I tried to talk in a friendly and interesting manner to a TV camera with an unconcerned cameraman behind it. I guessed I had probably done a pitiful job. I was surprised when Mr. Bell told me to report for work the following Monday. The salary was $5,000 per year, which was about what I earned in engineering three years earlier, but it was an increase from my Air Force salary.

As a KWTV meteorologist, I panned the weather instruments
to show current conditions.

I was given two weeks of training before I was allowed to go on the air live. They showed me how to put on makeup, how they wanted my hair cut, what kind of suit to wear, how to time my presentation around commercials, and how to imagine I was talking to a good friend just behind the camera. They gave me lessons about how to lower my voice, enunciate and appear at ease. These lessons continued for months after I was on the air live.

43

I was the second meteorologist behind Al Worth. Al was a talented broadcaster, but was not strong as a meteorologist. He helped me with television broadcasting and I helped him with forecasting Oklahoma weather. We were a good team. I did three morning shows and one noon show on weekdays plus two evening shows on Saturdays. Al presented all of the evening shows except Saturdays. I frequently substituted for him in addition to my 22 regular shows per week.

I liked television broadcasting, but was never quite satisfied with it. Mr. Bell insisted that his "personalities" stay around the station most of the day so they could give tours to visiting groups and help with public relations. I had trouble thinking of myself as a television "personality." I very much enjoyed the challenge of forecasting and the interface with viewers who phoned or stopped by the station to talk to me. I liked being asked to speak to clubs and schools. But I hated it when people recognized me on the street and asked me for an autograph. I felt like an imposter.

GRADUATE SCHOOL

I heard from Larry Davis that he had just been awarded a research assistantship at Penn State, working for Dr. Charles Hosler, our former meteorological instruments professor. I applied also. Dr. Hosler responded by mail, saying he could use me at the beginning of the second semester, in January 1961, if I would help him with the daily weather broadcast he was doing.

I had not been on television long enough to save much money. The assistantship would pay even less than we had made as an Air Force second lieutenant. By then, we had baby twins and a four-year-old daughter. At least the car, furniture and the Lew Wentz Foundation loan were finally paid off. Earlene and I decided to go for it, hoping that we could squeak by somehow. We sold our second car and our equity in our house to give us a small amount of cash to start with. Les had stopped riding his Vespa motor scooter, so I borrowed it for cheap transportation at school.

We packed an incredible amount of stuff into a big U-Haul trailer.

Our tired old Plymouth could barely pull the load. We started our trip to Pennsylvania in an ice storm. The storm and bad luck made the trip last a week. We were tired and nearly broke when we pulled into State College. As we looked at the huge piles of dirty snow, we wondered if we had lost our minds when we decided to return to school.

Dr. Hosler had started a noon weather show that was broadcast from the Penn State campus over station WFBG at Altoona. He asked me to alternate with him on the program. I jumped at it because I was still interested in broadcast meteorology. I continued doing the program for three years. It paid nothing, but it was excellent exposure and it enabled me to do other useful things.

One result of the weather program was that I was invited to take two courses in television broadcasting as electives. The first course, dealing with theoretical and practical aspects of broadcasting, required a term paper. I decided to do a paper comparing the ratings of weather shows presented by professional meteorologists compared to shows presented by non-meteorologists. Of the 512 VHF TV stations, only 32 used a meteorologist for presenting weather shows. I obtained the latest ARB ratings for the stations using professional meteorologists for the time of their weather shows plus the hour before and hour after the show. My statistical comparison of the ratings showed that the average ratings of the pairs of stations were nearly identical during the hour preceding the weather show. At the time of the weather show, the professional meteorologist station average ratings suddenly jumped up and the opposition lost an equal amount. The advantage for the professional station remained through the next hour. The effect was statistically significant.

Dr. Ken Spengler, Executive Director of the American Meteorological Society, heard about my paper and asked me to publish it in the AMS Bulletin. The paper was amazingly successful. In addition to the regular publication, the AMS mailed out thousands of copies over several years. Suddenly, and to my amazement, I was considered in meteorological circles to be an authority on television weather broadcasting. At an AMS meeting years later, Dr. Ken Spengler told me that my paper was still the most often requested paper of all time. As a result of it, the AMS offered me a position on the AMS professional staff at the end of my MS degree studies and again as I was finishing my PhD.

The second course was a practical course that was being organized by Professor Robert Greenfield, who had been the director of the Dinah Shore Show before joining the Penn State faculty. As a result of my paper, he offered to team with me in a special edition of his course that was designed especially to teach television weathercasting. There had never been such a course at any university up to that time. He taught the theoretical, artistic and practical aspects of television broadcasting. I taught the techniques for television interviewing and the production and presentation of news and weather shows. Students took turns operating the cameras, audio systems and lights. It turned out to be a very popular course for senior and graduate level meteorology students. Some of our students went on to become professional weathercasters.

Graduate Student

Dr. Hosler's cloud physics research project, on which I was employed, was funded by the National Science Foundation to study various aspects of the physics of clouds in central Pennsylvania. One interesting fact the project had already established was that average rainfall and hail patterns were oriented in bands parallel to the mountain ridges in central Pennsylvania. The ridges were oriented northeast-southwest and were quite regular, but were only about 800 feet above the valleys. There was no established meteorological theory to explain how 800-foot ridges could have such a dramatic effect on large storms.

I decided my thesis would be devoted to finding that link. I believed there had to be some mechanism whereby the vertical currents in the airflow over the mountains could be transmitted to at least 20,000-ft. altitude, where precipitation and hail are formed. Upward air currents should enhance precipitation and hail growth and downward air currents should decrease them, thus producing the precipitation and hail bands that had been observed.

I first had to characterize the airflow over the mountains in central Pennsylvania. Dr. Hosler's research program had acquired an Army surplus fire control radar, known as an M33. It had a powerful S-band (10 cm wavelength) radar that had been used by the Army to search for invading planes. It also had a good X-band (3 cm wavelength) tracking radar that had been used to track planes and provide aiming coordinates for anti-aircraft guns.

After a period of experimentation, I devised a balloon system that could rise to a desired level then float at that altitude except for being forced up and down by vertical air currents. Thus, the trajectory of the balloons could tell me the relation of vertical air currents to the mountains they were flying over. The tracking radar was a handy way to track the balloons and measure any vertical deviations from horizontal flight. I used wrinkled heavy duty aluminum foil as a reflector to hang beneath the balloons so the radar could track them.

One night, one of my balloons failed to rise as it was supposed to. It hit and created a short circuit between two high voltage power lines near the radar. The aluminum foil vaporized into a shower of colorful balls and a resounding BOOM. Immediately, the lights of the campus and most of the town went dark. I knew I was in trouble. A few days later, Dr. Hosler came walking down the hall with a bill for $10,000 in damage I had caused in the Penn State mushroom research facility. Thirty three years later, as Dr. Hosler was introducing me to an audience while I was being honored as a distinguished alumni, he remarked that I had been his most expensive graduate student.

It was difficult to find the right place to launch the balloons upwind so that they would fly over the terrain I wanted to study. I needed a means of making vertical air current measurements over a wider area and with better control of where the measurements would be made. I decided to use an airplane. Since I had my pilot's license, courtesy of the Air Force, I wanted to fly it myself.

I rented a Cessna 172 from a local fixed-base operator. I had not flown an aircraft since I earned my private license, four years earlier. I got a checkout in the Cessna 172 and flew around for two or three hours to get accustomed to the plane. I used the 172 to collect most of the data for my MS thesis

When I was ready to begin my measurement program, I happened to mention to Earlene that I was flying the plane. She threw a fit. She had gotten the idea from her father that flying is very dangerous. She had not liked my flying at A&M and did not want me flying in the Air Force. She thought her flying problem was over when we made the decision to drop out of the Air Force pilot training program. I was flying again, and she was mad. The best I could negotiate was a grudging agreement to continue as long as my thesis project required it.

I built a crude instrument system in the Cessna 172 and mounted it in place of the right front seat. The system recorded temperature, humidity, altitude and airspeed. The arrangement was very crude, but marginally sufficient for the purpose.

One of the most fundamental facts in meteorology is that dry air cools 5.5 degrees Fahrenheit per thousand feet when it rises and warms at the same rate when it sinks. I used this principle to compute the magnitude of rising and sinking air currents above the terrain. My airborne measurements were crude but they compared well with the balloon measurements. The airplane gave me the flexibility to make measurements anywhere. After months of tedious work, I was able to construct two dimensional airflow profiles above the mountain ridges in a variety of meteorological conditions.

A British meteorologist, Dr. R. S. Scorer, had developed a mathematical model that attempted to simulate the waves over mountains. I was delighted to find that the mountain waves and lee waves I measured fit the theory of Dr. Scorer very well. Since my measurements essentially confirmed his theory, it followed that I should be able to use his theory to predict mountain waves in conditions for which I was not able to make measurements. My equipment was too primitive to make measurements in a severe thunderstorm environment, so I needed a method to tie my measurements to thunderstorms if I was to explain the banded rainfall and hail patterns in

Pennsylvania.

It was well known by then that very severe thunderstorms are produced when a strong jet stream is overhead. When I applied Dr. Scorer's theory to the wind shear and stability of severe thunderstorms, I was able to show that waves in the environment of the thunderstorms were not only possible, but were very likely to form as thunderstorms pass over the Allegheny Mountains. Updrafts in the thunderstorms would be suppressed in downward moving parts of the mountain waves and encouraged in the upward moving parts. Thus, the updrafts strong enough to produce hail would be periodic as they pass over the ridges, leading to the hail bands parallel to the ridges.

Thus, I had established the link by which the relatively minor ridges in central Pennsylvania could transmit their influence to large thunderstorms. It was a new and surprising discovery in meteorology, and I felt thunderstorm experts would probably challenge it.

Severe Storms Paper

My MS thesis was well accepted by the Penn State faculty. Dr. Hosler told me the real test of my new discovery would be how the experts in the field would receive it. I decided to write a paper for the upcoming American Meteorological Society Severe Storms Conference to be held in Norman, Oklahoma. That was to be a major scientific conference, and the top severe storm scientists from around the world would be there.

I had never been to a scientific conference, and had never written a professional paper. The conference committee had announced that an award would be presented for the most significant paper on severe storms that year. Dr. Hosler said he thought I should be able to win with my paper, even though I was a beginner.

All of my public speaking contests and television shows failed to prepare me for the nervousness I felt when it came time to present my paper. I had only 10 minutes to give the paper. Fortunately my paper was printed in the published proceedings, which appeared before the conference, and most of the scientists had already read it. I got several good questions at the end of the paper.

I almost fell out of my seat when Dr. David Atlas, the conference chairman, announced that my paper had been selected as the most significant scientific contribution at the conference. I was surprised at the instant acceptance I received from the world's top scientists in the field of severe storms as a result of the paper. I developed numerous valuable friendships during that conference.

I was invited to write an expanded version of the paper for a Meteorological Monograph on severe storms, which was being developed by the AMS. Thus, my paper found a prominent and permanent place in a major work along with papers from the top experts in the field.

PhD Decision

We had originally planned to finish the MS degree, and then start a consulting business, probably as an adjunct to a TV career. By the time I earned my MS degree, our financial situation had improved and I was having considerable success in meteorology at Penn State. My consulting income brought our income up to about $7,000, 40% above my TV salary a year earlier. As a result of my television broadcast paper, severe storm paper, Dr. Hosler's influence and an expanding network of well-placed friends, I received several very desirable job offers. Dr. Hosler asked me to remain at Penn State to work on my PhD. I had dreamed about earning a PhD, but it never seemed possible before. By then, the idea seemed practical. Earlene and I decided we would stay on at Penn State so I could take a shot at the PhD. We were comfortable enough by then to buy a new Rambler station wagon and move to a two-bedroom house with a basement.

Bigger Aircraft

The success of the Cessna 172 for collecting meteorological data led to an opportunity to rent and use larger aircraft, a Cessna 205, and then a Cessna 210 for increasing data collection uses. I began thinking about acquiring a twin engine aircraft for the Meteorology Department.

I believed that I could develop a light twin engine aircraft with specialized instrumentation for the meteorology department. With Dr. Hosler's permission, I submitted a proposal to the National Science Foundation to acquire a new Piper Twin Comanche and cloud physics instrumentation for it. Much to the surprise of my professors, my proposal was funded. Since I had no multi-engine license and not enough hours to be approved for insurance, I hired an instructor to fly with me for the first 75 hours in the Twin Comanche. During that time, he helped me get my multi-engine and instrument licenses.

Earlene went with me on a trip to Fort Lauderdale, Florida for installation of turbochargers on the Twin Comanche. It was our first trip in an aircraft. Up to that point, she had not liked the idea of my flying research aircraft. She overcame her fear of flying when she could see that it was safe and enjoyable. We had a great week in the Florida sun while the turbochargers were installed and tested.

There was very little commercially available instrumentation for airborne cloud measurements at that time, so I had to build almost everything from scratch. I designed the instrument systems and the methods for installing them on the aircraft. Fortunately, Penn State had an excellent machine shop, so we could build just about anything we could dream up. After the instrumentation system was proven and calibrated, we were able to collect data on temperature, humidity, altitude, airspeed, cloud droplet sizes and images and other data that were considered important in cloud research. The instrumentation system was quite successful and was being noticed by researchers at other universities. It became the source for thesis data for several graduate students. I was happy to fly the aircraft for other graduate students and assist in getting the data they needed for their theses.

Radioactive Fallout Research

The US and the Soviet Union were finishing their respective atmospheric testing of atomic weapons, and there was much scientific and public worry about nuclear fallout, especially strontium-90, a very long lived and toxic radioactive element. It was showing up in milk from dairy cows. Nuclear Science and Engineering Co., of Pittsburg, had won a research contract to determine how strontium-90 was transported from the stratosphere onto dairy pastures. They hired Dr. Hosler as a consultant to do the research. He asked Larry Davis and me to help him with the research program.

Strontium-90 existed only in the stratosphere. Our job was to learn what downward transport mechanisms were involved in extracting strontium-90 from the stratosphere and depositing it on dairy pastures. We believed it had to come down with precipitation.

We decided that we would test rainwater for strontium-90 from different rain-producing systems, such as warm fronts, cold fronts, thunderstorms, etc. We would use the M33 radar and other data to analyze the precipitation generating mechanisms. We needed a way of collecting rainwater samples over a wide area during storms. I developed a rainwater-sampling network in central Pennsylvania using diaper buckets and children's plastic boats. Larry made arrangements for collecting radar data.

We used the M33 radar to collect data on the structure of the storms in which we collected the rainwater samples. Nuclear Science and Engineering Co. analyzed the samples to determine the radioactivity content. Larry and I worked with Dr. Hosler to correlate the radioactive content with our analyses of how the precipitation formed and reached the ground. We worked with Dr. Ed Danielson to develop isentropic analyses showing how the radioactivity was extracted from the stratosphere through a break in the tropopause at the jet stream location, then descended down frontal surfaces and became entrained into rain-generating clouds forming along the front. The remaining question concerned the possible role of thunderstorms reaching into the stratosphere on the deposition of radioactivity.

As a result of my severe storm paper and the work on radioactive fallout, Dr. Walter Saucier, head of the School of Meteorology at the University of Oklahoma asked me to set up a

M33 radar at Norman, Oklahoma and to join the Oklahoma University faculty. After thinking about it, I declined the faculty position but agreed to establish a M33 radar facility for him. Earlene and I moved temporarily to Norman so I could establish the radar system there.

I hired graduate students to help me set up the radar on the north edge of Westheimer Field at Norman. I used the radar to continue my work on radioactive fallout. I established a rainwater and hailstone collection network over most of Oklahoma. We used the radar to record data on the storms we collected rainwater samples from.

Nuclear scientists generally believed thunderstorms penetrating into the stratosphere would capture radioactive particles and bring them down with rain and hailstones, thus providing the mechanism for transporting strontium-90 from the stratosphere to the ground. However, we found that my rainwater and hailstones from very tall storms in Oklahoma contained no detectable amounts of strontium-90. This finding helped our team to develop a comprehensive theory about how radioactivity is transported from the stratosphere to the ground. We published our findings and our theory was generally accepted in the scientific community. A side benefit was that having used strontium-90 as a tracer, we had developed a fairly comprehensive theory on the interaction of the stratosphere and troposphere in general. This project could have been a very significant thesis topic.

Lightning Detector

During our two months in Norman, I became interested in measuring the intensity of thunderstorms by sensing the number of lightning strokes the thunderstorms produced. Larry Davis and I developed an idea that we could construct a dual channel AM radio receiver system that would detect the direction and distance of lightning strokes. Our idea was to use the relative strength at two radio frequencies to indicate the range of lightning strokes and a direction finding circuit to determine the direction of lighting strokes. We built a dual channel receiving system that used two crossed loop antennas mounted on top of the Mineral Industries building. We used an oscilloscope to display the direction and relative strength of lightning strokes. The device seemed to be fairly successful in displaying the direction and relative distance of lighting strokes.

Dr. Hosler walked in one day as we were playing with the device during a squall line passage. He said it was interesting, but he indicated it might be a good idea to think more about our own theses. I admitted that I was doing more interesting projects than I could manage. I dismantled the lightning detector and returned to my dissertation. A man named Ryan patented the idea a few years later and a built a substantial company around his "Stormscope." If we had carried our investigation a little further, we could have had the patent before Ryan did.

Weather Modification Research

Weather modification was a hotly debated subject in both public and scientific circles in those days. German scientists discovered in the 1930s that most precipitation forms in clouds at temperatures colder than freezing with a mixture of super-cooled liquid water droplets and ice crystals. The ice crystals take water from the liquid droplets, grow rapidly then fall in the form of snow or ice pellets. In the warm season, the snow or ice pellets melt and fall to the ground as rain. After World War II, a group of General Electric scientists discovered that one could increase precipitation in certain clouds by introducing a few more ice crystals into the clouds, thereby making more snow or ice pellets that then fall as snow or rain. Various methods of seeding clouds have been used to increase the ice content, including dry ice pellets or silver iodide crystals.

Soon after the General Electric studies were published, cloud seeding projects were started all around the world. Enthusiastic cloud seeders claimed great successes in increasing rainfall. Serious scientists in the 1950s began looking at the commercial cloud seeding projects and could find little evidence of statistically significant rainfall increases or decreases. By the time I became interested in the subject, there was widespread controversy, but very few serious research projects designed to settle the fundamental questions about the formation of precipitation.

Dr. Hosler, Larry Davis and I became interested in performing a few simple experiments in cloud seeding. Larry and I decided that a simple CO_2 fire extinguisher could be used to generate ice crystals in a super-cooled cloud, thereby increasing rainfall from it. We took a fire extinguisher from the lab one day when we observed a field of medium sized cumulus clouds in a fresh air mass from Canada. I flew the Cessna 172 to 13,000 feet to reach the -5C level. We picked a juicy looking cumulus and I penetrated it. Larry opened the window and discharged the fire extinguisher as we flew through the cloud. The airspeed meter dropped to zero on the second pass as the unheated pitot tube froze. I kept making crop duster turns and repeating penetrations using the sound of the slipstream to judge airspeed. We repeated the process 4 or 5 times. To our surprise, the cloud grew rapidly to well above 30,000 feet and produced a heavy shower. The radar data showed that our cloud was the only one in the state to produce a shower that day. We were very impressed with our success, and felt for a short while that scientific doubts about cloud seeding must be exaggerated. We reasoned that our seeding had caused massive freezing of liquid droplets, releasing 80 calories for each gram (the heat of fusion) of water frozen. This release of the heat of fusion increased the buoyancy of the cloud, causing it to go up like a hot air balloon. The growth then drew in fresh quantities of moist air that formed the shower we observed.

After the fire extinguisher experiment, Larry Davis, Charlie Hosler and I continued working on the theory that the most effective way to seed clouds would be to produce massive amounts of ice crystals suddenly in a large, wet updraft. Our calculations indicated that the resulting release of the heat of fusion would increase the updraft buoyancy by one to two degrees Celsius, thus making it grow faster and stimulating further updrafts that would resupply the super cooled water reservoir needed to generate rainfall. We believed that was what happened in our fire extinguisher experiment. Larry developed a computer model to prove the viability of this theory for his dissertation. His computations showed that the idea would work only in certain conditions, but that those conditions could be identified and exploited. Dr. Joanne Simpson, a NOAA scientist, developed the same general hypothesis at about the same time. She later initiated a project to test the theory in the field. Both Larry's model and Joanne's experiments indicated the method should be viable for wet tropical clouds, and might be viable for more temperate latitude clouds. This was a fairly radical new approach to cloud seeding theory and would stimulate yet another area of scientific and public debate about the whole idea of weather modification. .

Lucky Graduate Student

I was fortunate to have the position I did at Penn State. Dr. Hosler was able to attract well-funded research grants and consulting contracts. He was one of the more generous professors toward his graduate students. By doing much of the work on Dr. Hosler's projects, Larry and I had access to the best research equipment and on very rewarding consulting jobs. We were able to establish reputations of our own. When Dr. Hosler became the Head of the Department of Meteorology in 1961, Larry and I were given even greater freedom to pursue outside consulting jobs, and to write our own proposals and scientific papers. Larry and I were regarded as the entrepreneurs of the graduate school. Dr. Panofsky always called me "the tycoon."

Family Life in State College

We managed to have a reasonably normal family life in State College in spite of my very long work hours. We were able to travel around Pennsylvania and to Washington or New York once in a while. We made occasional trips back to Oklahoma. Karen started school in State College. The boys learned to play at just about anything available. They loved sliding on snow down the hill behind our house in a couple of plastic boats left over from my radioactive rain collection network. Mom came for a visit and we took her to Rehoboth Beach for her first sight of the ocean.

One day, while I was at the airport, I received the chilling news that Earlene had been in an accident and that I could find her at the doctor's office. When I got there, I found her with a broken clavicle, a goose egg on her head and a wounded knee. The boys, who had been in the back of the station wagon, were skinned up, but OK. Earlene had been driving our new Rambler and was hit broadside by a lady who ran a stop sign. The car remained upright, but was badly bent.

Since bad luck seems to come in streaks, I should not have been surprised to learn a week later that Larry had stood up on his stroller and fell off, breaking his clavicle in the same place as Earlene's. For weeks, two of the family wore figure 8 bandages.

Teaching

Dr. Hosler offered me a chance to teach a course in introductory meteorology. I taught the course two semesters before my research and consulting load became too heavy to continue teaching.

Our family at Penn State in 1964

Near the end of my PhD studies, Dr. Hosler offered me the course in meteorological instrumentation, which he had taught for many years. It was a popular course, so I had about 75 students. I devoted a substantial portion of the course content to new systems being introduced then, such as meteorological satellites, small computers for modeling and radar data processing. I taught the course only one semester because of the need to devote time to my dissertation.

I found teaching to be very enjoyable, and I could see that I would like a teaching career. When a professorship was offered to me, I was very tempted to take it.

57

Finishing at Penn State

In late 1964, Earlene and I began thinking seriously about what we wanted to do. We had numerous opportunities then. The American Meteorological Society still wanted me to join the staff and promote professional activities. Dr. Paul MacCready offered me a job as a research meteorologist at his Altadena-based Meteorology Research, Inc. Penn State and the University of Oklahoma offered me jobs as a professor of meteorology. There were interesting opportunities in NOAA, in Washington. Neither of us was eager to raise our family in Boston, Los Angeles or Washington. The Penn State job sounded good, except that we were not fond of living in Pennsylvania either. The University of Oklahoma had a young meteorology school, but it would be many years before it would become a first rate meteorology school.

During 1963 and 1964, I was able to build a small business selling weather forecasts related to snow making for several ski slopes in the Northeast. However, I had since become more interested in meteorological instrumentation and research aircraft. I decided to abandon my forecast business so I could concentrate on building scientific research aircraft. I offered all of my ski slope accounts to Joel Myers, a younger graduate student, who showed an interest in forecasting. He formed a company called AccuWeather, Inc. The business I gave Joel grew to employ hundreds of meteorologists within a few years.

Because of my involvement in so many projects and teaching, I was not able to finish my dissertation before we moved away from Penn State in the spring of 1965. I planned to finish it while I worked in South Dakota. However, I still did not have it finished by the end of the summer of 1965. I had a difficult decision to make. We had already moved the company and our family from Penn State to Norman, Oklahoma. Earlene and I decided that we would put our new company on hold while I returned to Penn State alone to finish my dissertation. I rented a room and concentrated on writing and defending the dissertation for two months. Finally, it was done. I was awarded a PhD in December 1965, several months after we had moved to Oklahoma.

THIRD QUARTER - CAREER

WEATHER SCIENCE, INC.

New Company

Penn State always had lots of visits from prominent research meteorologists. By late 1964, several visiting meteorological research program managers from around the country had seen the Twin Comanche instrumentation system and expressed interest in having me build one for them. Dr. Richard Schleusener, the Director of the Institute of Atmospheric Sciences at the South Dakota School of Mines and Technology at Rapid City was the most serious. In November 1964, I signed a $65,000 contract with the SDSM&T. Dr. Schleusener asked me to build two instrumentation systems, one for a twin engine airplane, which I would furnish, and one for his North American T6. Thus, the Twin Comanche was the springboard from which our first company, Weather Science, Inc., was launched.

The Twin Comanche and instrument systems that made our new company possible.

We called our new company Weather Science, Inc. Neither of us had taken a business course or had any experience in operating a business. Earlene hired an accountant to set up books for the company and teach her how to keep records. She handled the money management part of the business from our living room. I handled the technical part of the business from our basement. That arrangement survived more than 25 years.

We had about $400 in the bank. Our new contract was our only real asset. I gave Mr. Wise, Vice President Citizen's National Bank, a copy of the contract and told him that I needed to borrow all of the money required to buy an airplane and to perform on the contract, but I had no collateral. I was still a graduate student at the time. Mr. Wise said something about how other high technology companies in State College had started on a shoestring and had grown to be very prosperous. He said we might be another successful upstart, so I got the loan. Even though his name was Wise, I'm not sure how wise he was.

For the South Dakota project, I needed a turbocharged aircraft that could penetrate large cumulus clouds at 20,000 feet altitude. Turbocharging was rare in light aircraft at that time, so there weren't many choices. I selected a three-year-old Piper Apache that belonged to Pug Piper, the son of Bill Piper, the founder of Piper Aircraft. Pug had turbochargers installed on his personal aircraft to see if they wanted to incorporate them in new aircraft from the factory. I paid $30,000 for the Apache. I had barely 250 hours flying time then.

We had no shop, no tools and no employees. We had to acquire everything we needed from scratch. I set up a crude shop of our 10 by 12-foot basement that served as a laundry, utility and storage room. I hired three of the Penn State project engineering staff to work evenings and weekends on our new instrument system. All of us worked very long hours to produce the instrument systems in four months. When we finished the instrumentation console for the twin engine aircraft, there wasn't room to get it off the workbench, so we dismantled the bench to get the console out of the basement.

No heated hangars were available in State College, so I rented an old broken down T hangar from Sherm Lutz, who ran a grass landing strip south of State College. We draped a plastic tent over the plane to slow down the frigid wind that blew through the many cracks in the hangar. We heated the tent with a kerosene heater. It nearly asphyxiated us. The experience of modifying the aircraft and installing the instrument system in such crude and harsh conditions was a factor in our decision to move the company away from State College.

Move to Norman

When we formed the company, we had to make a decision about where we would live after finishing at Penn State. The easiest course was to remain in State College. But, we knew that we would probably be stuck there permanently once we hired full time employees and moved into permanent quarters. We were not fond of State College as a place to live. I disliked working on airplanes in the terrible winter weather there. The most likely potential customers we could identify were in California, South Dakota, Oklahoma and Colorado. We felt we would do better if we were closer to our potential customers.

Dr. Schleusener pressured us to move to Rapid City. He promised that we would be the prime contractor for his growing research project there. He even offered me a leadership position in the Institute of Atmospheric Sciences. However, Rapid City was a remote location and I knew it would be an even worse place than State College to work on airplanes during the winter. A move to either Boulder or Norman seemed the best of the available options. We decided on Norman because (1) we had become well acquainted with the town, (2) it looked like our next contract would probably come from the National Severe Storms Laboratory at Norman, and (3) we would be closer to our families at Norman.

In late April, when the instrument systems were finished, it was time for me to depart in the Apache to spend the rest of the summer flying on a research project at Rapid City, South Dakota. After the movers picked up all of our furniture, Earlene and the children headed for Oklahoma in the station wagon. I departed in the Apache for South Dakota. Earlene took complete charge of moving and establishing a new home and office in a new town.

I was able to fly to Norman a few times that summer when breaks in the weather coincided with weekends. Earlene and the children visited Rapid City for about a week that summer. It was the first time since returning to Penn State that we could really relax and play together. We explored every corner of the Black Hills and Badlands, attended rodeos and generally had a great time. It was a valuable time in the development of our young family.

Penetrating Cumulus Clouds

Our South Dakota School of Mines contract required us to support cloud research work for the Bureau of Reclamation. The Bureau had established an office in Denver to study means of enhancing water resources in 17 western states through cloud seeding. A major scientific question for weather modification in those days concerned the population of ice crystals produced naturally in cumulus clouds.

The main theory of cloud seeding that had prevailed since the late 1940s became known as the "static seeding" theory. It held that cumulus clouds contained abundant amounts of super cooled water with too few ice particles for efficient production of rainfall. If that were true, we could increase rainfall by increasing the number of ice crystals contained in the super cooled water cloud.

Our first aircraft with instruments and camera for making cloud penetrations.

However, Dr. Roscoe Braham at the University of Chicago had found that ice crystals were overly abundant in most cumulus clouds in Missouri and Minnesota. If his finding were confirmed for cumulus clouds elsewhere, the entire theory of "static seeding" could be invalidated.

Dick Schleusener asked me to do a study to see if Dr. Braham's results applied in South Dakota. I was to determine the ice particle population of cumulus clouds in various meteorological situations using methods similar to Dr. Braham's. The future of his cloud seeding research project depended on the outcome. Our method was to fly the Apache into tall cumulus clouds at the altitude of the minus 5C isotherm to measure liquid water content and ice crystal populations. If the static seeding theory was valid, we should find clouds at that level to be made up of super cooled water with few ice crystals present. If we found large numbers of ice crystals, the whole static seeding theory would be seriously in doubt.

Liquid water content of clouds was relatively easy to measure. Ice crystal content was much more difficult. No accepted method for doing so had been established. Dr. Braham had used a tube facing into the airstream to bring ice crystals into the cabin for counting and inspection. He also used Formvar-coated film to capture and make replicas of ice particles. Using his idea, I installed a two inch diameter copper tube extending forward from the cabin through the stubby Apache nose so it looked directly into the airstream. We counted the ice crystals coming into the cabin in a manner similar to what Dr. Braham had done. We used Formvar coated microscope slides to make replicas of the particles, which we stored on dry ice for later microscopic examination. John Hirsch, my observer, used a tape recorder to record his observations of number and ice particle type.

We penetrated 365 tall, rapidly growing cumulus clouds during the summer of 1965. My technique was to set up a steady level flight at about 90 knots and fly a constant pitch attitude and power setting once I reached the cloud. We used the updraft-induced rate of climb as a measure of the updraft strength and diameter. The aircraft picked up considerable ice during penetrations, so we frequently had to descend below the freezing level to shed the ice load, and then climb back up for more penetrations.

I learned a great deal about updrafts that was not in any of the meteorological literature. I found that the broad updrafts were very smooth in the middle, but with very strong, sometimes violent, turbulence at the edges, especially on the upwind side. The updraft speeds in the broad updrafts were frequently in excess of 6,000 feet per minute. We sometimes found ourselves going up almost as fast as we were moving horizontally. It seemed very unnatural to see the altimeter winding rapidly and the rate of climb pegged while flying in a smooth, quiet updraft. We learned that the easiest path through the updrafts was perpendicular to the environmental wind direction.

The Apache proved to be a good aircraft for cumulus cloud penetrations, in spite of its poor performance. It had a strong wing and it was very easy to fly. I could maintain good lateral control down to stall speed. I was never in danger of losing control of the plane, even in violent turbulence.

One day, while Earlene was visiting Rapid City, John Hirsch was not available to fly as observer, so I asked Earlene to be my observer. I showed her how to prepare Formvar microscope slides, catch ice particle samples on the slides, and count the ice crystals coming through the nose tube. As we approached the first cloud, she stared in horror and disbelief at the rapidly boiling mass of cloud ahead of us. She looked at me like she thought I was playing some sort of trick and said "you're not planning to go into THAT are you?". She was clearly scared out of her wits as we entered the cloud and hit the first strong gust. She was holding on with both hands and forgot to capture and count ice crystals. Suddenly, we hit a high concentration of graupel, or small ice pellets. A shower of ice pellets bounced all over the cockpit. I almost laughed myself silly as she began chasing the pellets around the cockpit, trying to get one on a microscope slide. After a few more penetrations, she settled down and became a good observer. She told me after the flight that she still thought I was completely crazy for deliberately flying into such violent clouds.

That summer, we learned that most isolated cumulus clouds in the northern Great Plains, as they rise through the -5C level, were almost pure super cooled water, with very few ice particles present. However, such isolated clouds usually had entrained too much dry air and were not suitable for seeding anyway. Most clouds thought to be candidates for seeding were part of a larger cloud complex. We found that growing cumulus towers that touch an older and taller tower almost always contained heavy concentrations of ice crystals at the -5C level, so they would be poor candidates for "static" seeding. We also found that cumulus growing under an old cirrus cloud was likely to have high concentrations of ice crystals. Those results suggested that seeding to add more ice nuclei in the clouds where already abundant ice particles were found would only be counterproductive. We were able to find a sufficient number of cumulus in which a brief opportunity for static seeding seemed to exist. However, my interest in the "dynamic" seeding hypothesis we had developed at Penn State increased.

Tornado Research

In 1965, very little was known about the dynamics of tornadic

Our first Aztec with balloon launching tubes being loaded with a super-pressure balloon for a tornado hunting mission.

storms. Doppler weather radar had not yet been developed. The National Severe Storms Laboratory (NSSL) had just been established on Westheimer Field at Norman to study severe storms, especially tornadic storms and was open to new ideas. I made an appointment to see the new NSSL director, Dr. Edwin Kessler. I described my idea for making measurements of the air currents in tornadic storms using radar-tracked balloons. My idea was to develop a version of my Penn State balloons that I could launch from an aircraft into the inflow to tornadic storms. The balloons would carry a tiny radar transponder that would enable the M33 radar to track the balloons, even in very dense storms. Ed thought my idea was a very long shot, but would think about it.

I continued working on the idea as I returned to Penn State in the fall of 1965 to finish my dissertation. I discussed it with Bob Cook, who had helped build our first instrumentation systems, and was familiar with the M33 radar. At first, Bob didn't think the idea would work, but he agreed to build a prototype of the circuit I had in mind so we could test it using the Penn State M33 radar. The experiment was successful and proved that my idea might be feasible.

I hired Bob to design the transponder and a companion receiver for the M33 radar that I had installed in Norman two years earlier. I needed it to weigh less than 100 grams and cost less than $40 in quantity. I estimated that a launcher for a balloon capable of carrying a 100 gram transponder would be feasible for a Piper Aztec, Cessna 310 or Beech Twin Bonanza. NSSL gave me a contract to develop the balloon-transponder system in time for the tornado season of 1966.

I was anticipating a contract for hailstorm research in South Dakota for the summer of 1966. For that, I would need an aircraft capable of operating above 18,000 feet. Piper Aircraft had just introduced a turbocharged version of the Piper Aztec. I decided to try to buy one to use as a balloon launcher in the spring and for hailstorm research aircraft in the summer. The risk for buying the Aztec was very high, since the hail research contract was still a bird in the bush and the tornado contract alone could not support the aircraft. We were new in Norman and it was difficult to negotiate a $65,000 loan for a plane to fly around tornadoes and hailstorms. We made a deal at a very high rate of interest with a bank in Norman that we later learned was run by a man of very questionable character. After making the loan, he thought he owned me.

My idea was to use a cylindrical balloon made of clear Mylar that could carry the small radar transponder. I wanted to be able to launch up to three of the balloon-transponders on one flight. The design and fabrication of the balloons and a balloon launcher proved to be difficult. My design involved fabricating a sausage shaped Mylar balloon that could be housed inside cylindrical tubes mounted on the Aztec belly. The launching tubes had to be nearly air-tight in order to protect the balloon from the slipstream. Yet, the launcher had to be able to release the balloon-transponder assembly quickly and without damage to the fragile material.

The final transponder design weighed 72 grams. The balloon required to carry it was nine feet long and sixteen inches diameter and could barely fit under the belly of our new Piper Aztec. The three launcher tubes lacked only four inches touching the ground with the struts pumped all the way up. All of my persuasive powers were needed to convince the FAA inspector to let me fly the launcher.

By April 1966, the balloon, launcher, transponder and radar were working reasonably well. I flew the Aztec around violent storms for six weeks in search of a tornado, but was unable to find one within the tracking range of the M33 radar. We launched numerous balloons into thunderstorm updrafts and gained considerable data that would be useful as a basis of comparison for later tornado measurements. One of our interesting findings was a balloon launched near the ground was more likely to be entrained into a storm than one launched near the cloud base. The air feeding the updrafts comes from near the ground. Thus, to get balloons into the tornado vortex, we learned that we would need launch at low altitude and close to the storm.

It was the spring of 1967 before we finally found a tornado in a suitable location. We launched a balloon after dark just north of the radar site. It was drawn rapidly northward and into the vortex of a tornadic storm that moved across Midwest City. We tracked the balloon through the updraft to about 45,000 feet. That was, as far as I have ever learned, the first physical measurement of the updraft trajectory in a tornadic storm.

Hailstorm Research

While I was working in South Dakota in 1965, I helped Dick Schleusener promote a multi-agency cooperative hail research project to be conducted near Rapid City in the summer of 1966. The idea gained generally good acceptance in the scientific community, so the National Science Foundation decided to fund it. To my great relief, we were invited to participate with our new Aztec.

I had promoted a plan to penetrate growing towers at the -5C level (about 18,000 feet) with an aircraft equipped about like the Apache, but with a new instrument for recording ice and water particle concentrations. I had been tinkering with piezo-electric transducers, which I believed could be used to measure the mass of precipitation particles. I designed an instrument that I called the "rain rate meter" using a piezo-electric transducer. The instrument produced a voltage pulse proportional to the momentum of the particle striking the exposed surface. By dividing out true airspeed, I could compute the mass spectra and concentration of particles in the volume swept out by the transducer. I mounted my first model on the nose of the Piper Aztec. I was delighted to see that the shape of voltage pulses from water droplets were different from those produced by ice particles. That fact suggested that I could develop a way to electronically differentiate pulses produced by water and ice particles. The recording system was crude, so data processing was slow and very labor intensive, but the results were very useful.

The second idea I had promoted was an armored aircraft that would be capable of penetrating directly into the hail forming zones of thunderstorms. I proposed a much more robust version of my rain-rate meter for measuring hailstone impacts. I proposed using a Navy surplus T28 aircraft with special armor plating over all leading edges. The canopy would be reinforced with thick Acrylic that would be capable of withstanding four inch hailstones. All reviewers thought it was a good idea. However, Paul MacCready, my old friend from Meteorology Research, Inc., outmaneuvered me and got that part of the job. Unfortunately, he left MRI before the work started and the job was turned over to another engineer. The job was very late and very much over budget. I could have done a much better job. The armored T28 was used for many years and many of my instrument designs were incorporated on it.

Our participation in the hail research project was very successful. We soon learned of other projects on which the Aztec could be used, giving me some assurance that I would be able to make the payments on it.

Growing Research Support Business

The Bureau of Reclamation established a new research center at the Fresno State College in 1965. It was to concentrate on technology for increasing the snowpack in the high Sierras during winter storms. I was able to sell Fresno State a project to provide the Aztec and our instrumentation systems in support of their research. A winter project was absolutely necessary if I was to make the payments on the Aztec. We provided aircraft support for Fresno State research for four winters. Our role was to provide technical support, not to participate directly in the research effort.

I made a deal to provide technical support for the University of Wyoming's weather modification research project on Elk Mountain. Dr. Don Veal asked us to build a version of our Aztec instrumentation system for his Twin Beech.

Dr. Pete Sinclair, of Colorado State University, asked me to furnish an instrumented Twin Comanche for his cloud research at the CSU. Pete found the Twin Comanche to be too small in 1966, so he contracted with us for an Aztec and a larger instrument system in 1967.

By the end of our first year in business at Norman, we were building our sixth airborne meteorological system, providing research support for four universities and making balloons and radar transponders for several customers. Our staff had grown to about a dozen and everybody was very busy.

Big Surprise

In September 1966, I gave a paper at a scientific meeting at Page, Arizona. I talked about the implications of our South Dakota ice particle concentration data on the static seeding and the possible alternative of the dynamic seeding hypothesis that we had worked on at Penn State. I pointed out that the static seeding theory seemed to be limited to only a few isolated cumulus towers. I suggested that the dynamic seeding idea might be more effective in clouds with high water contents. To be effective, I said a system for massive seeding would be required. After my talk, a distinguished looking gentleman with a gray beard approached me and said bluntly that he would give me a contract someday. I was startled and hardly knew what to say. He introduced himself as Dr. Pierre St. Amand, head of a research and development unit at the China Lake Naval Air Station. He would give no hint as to what he had in mind.

Late in the afternoon of December 26 1966, Pierre called me and asked if I could be in his office at 8AM the next morning. I said I could if it was important. He assured me it was. I flew the Aztec to California that evening.

When I walked into Pierre's office, he looked squarely at me and said that he could not tell me anything unless I could promise that I could produce an Aztec with a full instrumentation system and a second aircraft with seeding racks for an overseas deployment in 10 days. Four men, two in Navy uniforms, were looking at me, and waiting for an answer. I remembered that I had committed the Aztec and its instrumentation system plus Lynn Cooper to Fresno State and we had committed Augie Auer and other instrumentation to the University of Wyoming for the winter. I thought that, if it were important enough, I could probably get them back. I said yes, I could.

Pierre and the others then took me into a secure room to brief me. They told me that US Secretary of State Dean Rusk and Secretary of Defense Robert McNamara had just authorized a high priority and highly classified program to take China Lake's cloud seeding technologies to India. They planned to cooperate with Indian scientists to try to break a severe drought that had affected that country for more than two years. They told me that the very existence of the project and everything about it was classified at a very high level. The project had the code name Gromet. I would be able to use that name, but not be able to reveal our destination or our purpose to anyone, including the people I would take with me. He said he would tell our people about our purpose and destination just before we board an Air Force transport and that nobody would be able to communicate with home during the project. They said they had no time to get me a Top Secret clearance, but I would be held personally liable as though I had it. I said I would need to borrow money to buy airplanes and equipment, and asked them what I should tell my banker. The Navy captain gave me his name and phone number and said to have my banker call him if he had any questions.

Pierre said they would need an Aztec with my rain rate meter on it, and with the best weather radar I could get. They also wanted me to furnish a Cessna 206 with cloud seeding equipment. I tried not to let my face show the fact that I had not the slightest idea how I would produce all of that stuff in 10 days. Effectively I had no aircraft, no instrumentation and no people that were not already committed for the winter, and much of what the Navy wanted was special-order anyway.

Some people from Contracts then joined us. They asked me what the effort would cost. There was no choice but to pull numbers right out of the air. Within two hours, we had a preliminary contract total and they said they would start processing the contract, and they verbally authorized me to proceed. Before noon, I was driving off the base to start work, and I had not one shred of paper to prove that I had ever even talked to anybody at China Lake, much less have any sort of contract commitment. They could later have denied they talked to me and I would surely have been committed to a mental institution for rehabilitation.

I was never briefed on the real reason for the project. However, I was exposed to data and conversations that enabled me to put the beyond-Top-Secret pieces together. I never hinted to anyone until after the project had been declassified that I had any idea what the real purpose of Gromet was.

The Viet Nam war was heating up strongly then. The Viet Cong were transporting supplies and weapons on foot and by truck down the Ho Chi Mihn Trail. It was like a stream of ants, each carrying only a tiny crumb, but the final total was enough to supply an army. Interruption of this supply line was a most urgent priority in the war effort. Listening devices were planted along the Ho Chi Mihn Trail and aerial surveillance was used to try to find targets to shoot at, but the effectiveness of the foot soldier supply line was not seriously diminished. We were part of an effort to try something new – flood the rivers to slow the traffic.

Pierre had suggested that cloud seeding to make rain and flood the rivers along the Ho Chi Mihn Trail would be an effective way to slow the Viet Cong supply system. Flooded rivers were considered an effective barrier to Viet Cong supply lines. Pierre reasoned that making floods was a far more humane way to fight a war than using napalm and bombs. Pierre had been developing pyrotechnic devices for seeding hurricanes during the past several years. While the devices were experimental, laboratory tests indicated they should be very effective in producing massive amounts of ice crystals in super cooled clouds. His pyrotechnic devices were ideally suited for the dynamic seeding theory I had discussed in my paper at Page, Arizona.

Quantitative measurements of the results of massive seeding in large, wet cumulus were needed. Pierre liked the airborne rain rate meter I described in my paper for making airborne measurements of the amount of rain produced by cumulus clouds. The rain rate meter looked like an attractive way of evaluating a cloud seeding project in an area where few ground-based measurements were possible.

Pierre needed a place where wet clouds similar to those in Viet Nam could be seeded to test his pyrotechnic devices and their effectiveness in producing rainfall. He decided that India would be a good site because the monsoon clouds fit the requirements and the protracted drought there would provide a good cover story. The real purpose of Project Gromet could be disguised under the cover of a humanitarian effort by the United States to counter the effects of the drought in India. The need for secrecy could be explained by the natural awkwardness of having a military organization involved in cloud seeding. They believed the Indians could be counted upon to keep the existence of Project Gromet a secret. The involvement of the US military was to be concealed by using civilians to do the work. I was to lead the civilians.

The Buildup

After I told Earlene about what I had gotten us into, she took on the first challenge of contacting our people, who were scattered around the US on a Christmas vacation. We had to get everybody back to work but we could tell them little or nothing about why it was urgent. Their reactions were interesting. Augie Auer came back with a testy attitude. When he heard that the reason he was called back to work had to do with a military project with very tight security requirements, he was offended and would do nothing to help with the project. Others were excited to be involved in something that sounded so important,

Cessnas being loaded on a C141 for the trip to India.

and worked night and day to get the job done.

For various reasons, we found that the assets we had committed to Fresno and Wyoming were not available for the upcoming project, so we had to buy two new aircraft and outfit them with new instrumentation. We needed additional personnel very quickly. We recruited people from the list of friends we had made in the past few years and were able to assemble a reasonably competent crew in a very short time.

Our most urgent priority was to find enough money to buy a new Piper Aztec and a Cessna 206 plus the radar and other equipment required for the project. We knew by then that our original banker was not to be trusted. We were barely acquainted with Jack Patton, the owner and President of the Security National Bank. Why should he make a 100% loan to a near stranger for aircraft and equipment to go to an undisclosed overseas location and do something we could not talk about?

Jack Patton seemed delighted to see me as he waved me to a chair and sat down behind his big desk in the corner of the bank. I told Jack what I could about Project Gromet and how we needed to buy two planes immediately, equip them and take them to an undisclosed overseas location. Jack noted that this was quite different from his usual loan requests, which were more commonly for cows or hay. As he leaned back in his chair and looked up at the ceiling, I decided it was time to give him the name of the Navy captain who had said I should have our banker call if we needed to. He took the name and I left. The next day, Jack was ready to do business. I was very surprised and relieved to get the loan under those circumstances from a banker who hardly knew us.

We had problems getting insurance for the planes. Since we could not disclose our destination or activity, our insurance company charged us an astronomical fee of $10,000 for insurance on the two planes for six months. The Navy approved the cost without a whimper.

The days and nights during this period were intensively involved in expediting everything from passports to aircraft modifications, while continuing support for Fresno State and Wyoming. Earlene got two engineers out of a New Year's Eve party to begin work on a custom radome for the Aztec. Such extraordinary measures were necessary in order to meet our

74

almost unachievable mobilization goals. We were thankful that the deployment was delayed until January 19th. Our crew and equipment were at China Lake, ready to deploy at the appointed hour.

Our deployment crew heard about our purpose and destination for the first time from Pierre just before boarding an Air Force C141 at China Lake. Another contractor, Lee Wilson, was there with his crew of pilots and mechanics. I could see that his people already knew all about the project and had talked about it with their families. A third contractor, Tom Henderson, had evidently observed the security procedures just as we had.

Four Cessnas and project equipment were loaded on an Air Force C141 in a very unconventional manner that caused considerable squabbling with the crew who was to fly it. There was so little room that many of us were told to ride on mattresses under the aircraft. The C141 flew directly to New Delhi with only brief fuel stops and crew changes at San Francisco and Wake Island. I had contracted with a ferry pilot to fly our new Aztec to New Delhi.

India

We arrived at the New Delhi Palaam Airport about daybreak. We quickly unloaded the planes and equipment on the ramp beside a row of Soviet-made MIGs. Before the end of the day, we had installed the wings on all four Cessnas and moved everything to a hangar that had been prepared for us at the old Safdarjung Airport.

We were given VIP treatment. We were furnished a fleet of cars and drivers at each of our operating bases. We were entertained by very high officials in the Indian government. The leaders of the project were frequently invited to dinner at the home of Ambassador Chester Bowles. On days off, we toured the Taj Majal and many other centuries-old wonders.

The contrasts in India were dramatic. Most Indians walked, rode bicycles or rode in carts pulled by very small horses, while the privileged few tore down the streets in chauffeur-driven cars with horns honking. Cattle roamed the streets and could not be butchered because they were considered holy, while children died of starvation on the same streets.

At every stop, we were surrounded by children, many obviously malnourished, begging for money or food. I helped ship one of Pierre's people home after he had a mental breakdown due to the stress of seeing starving children. We saw funeral processions carrying the dead to the sacred waters of the Ganges River for cremation. We saw bodies being cremated on open fires along the banks of the Ganges.

We sat cross legged on little custom mats and drank tea with our Indian hosts while they bought fine silks and potteries at auction. I listened to commitments of young Indian men who pledged to have only one child, and to be sterilized after their first child or have their wife get an abortion if there was another pregnancy. I saw the widespread acceptance of a government program to give a transistor radio to any man who would have himself sterilized.

Gromet I

After briefings at the embassy and with our Indian hosts, we were allowed to begin operations. However, the long and severe drought was still at full strength, and there were no suitable clouds to work with. During the lull, I developed friendships with scientists and administrators in the Indian Meteorological

Our second Aztec with cloud seeding equipment and instrumentation over India.

Service. I learned that the Indian scientists had operated a warm cloud (clouds warmer than freezing) seeding research project for several years and had moderate hopes for good statistical results. Their project involved releasing very fine salt particles from ground-based dispensers at locations near the edge of the Rajasthan Desert. They had a generally poor opinion of cold cloud seeding with silver iodide, but were interested in the theory of massive seeding we were hoping to employ in their tropical cumulus clouds. There was also considerable interest in the cloud and precipitation measurements we would make.

Finally, monsoon moisture began arriving in the Ganges Valley, and a few workable clouds began appearing. We were required at first to have an Indian scientist aboard our aircraft for all flights. Dr. R. C. Shrivastava and Dr. B. H. V. Ramana Murty, two senior scientists with whom I had developed a friendship, were assigned to fly with me for our first seeding flight into

With Pierre St. Amand in India.

cumulus near New Delhi. I expected one of them to sit up front with me, but they insisted on sitting together in the two middle seats. I found an area of rapidly growing cumulus clouds that looked suitable for seeding. I began penetrating them and firing fusees to seed them. After the first penetration through one of the larger cumulus, I looked back to see my two friends holding hands, afraid for their lives. I made a couple more passes and returned to Safdarjung Airport. My friends vanished quickly.

The next time I was to fly, no Indian scientist could be found to accompany me. They were not about to get into another of our aircraft. Since time was critical, I decided to take off anyway. Soon after takeoff, I received a radio call, asking if there was an Indian aboard. At that time, I believed what I had heard from Dad and Grandpa Booker, that there was American Indian blood in our family. After a second or two of thinking, I replied "Yes, there's an Indian aboard." Pierre roared with laughter when he heard the story later that day. He was still telling that story when I last saw him. Soon, the requirement for an Indian to be aboard all flights was withdrawn.

Dr. Pierre St. Amand was my boss. While I ran most of the technical aspects of the project, he maintained the official interface with the Indian government and with our own

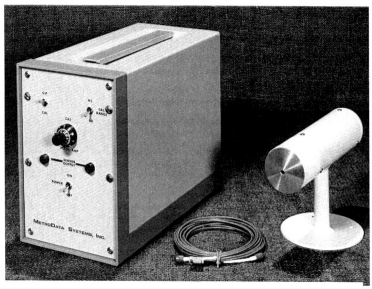

The rain rate sensor and digitizer that was used extensively in cloud seeding research.

government. He was a very forceful and outspoken man who had the ability to communicate effectively with low ranking sailors or high ranking diplomats. He regarded the development of pyrotechnics for massive seeding of clouds, and its potentially critical influence on the outcome of the Viet Nam war, to be one of the most important works of his illustrious career. He had been raised as the son of a French fur trader in an Eskimo village in Alaska. After a very late start, he had achieved a BS degree at the University of Alaska and his PhD at the California Institute of Technology. His formal education was mainly in geophysics and he was well known as an expert on earthquakes. He delighted in developing new, innovative and controversial theories and selling them to a variety of audiences. He was a leader in the development of the Sidewinder, the first heat-seeking air-to-air missile. His meteorological education was self taught.

His partnership with me was unique. He had tremendous personal magnetism and extraordinary scientific intuition to go with well-demonstrated persuasive abilities. Yet, the established cloud physics scientific community treated him with suspicion and disdain. To accomplish his goals, he needed a scientist who could communicate effectively with the scientific community. I had established a solid relationship with that community. Pierre's pyrotechnics were very effective in producing massive amounts of ice in cumulus clouds. That fact was central to the dynamic seeding hypothesis we had developed at Penn State. Our partnership had the potential to produce something very significant.

I felt that there must be some way to use Pierre's great achievement in pyrotechnics development with solid cloud physics theory and measurements to accomplish results that would be accepted ultimately in the scientific world. If I could work effectively with this opportunity, I felt it would be a milestone in the history of meteorology, and therefore worthy of my all-out effort.

The practical aspects of an operation in India were almost overwhelming. The Indians had taken a very bureaucratic form of government left by the British and make it much worse. Every flight required a flight plan, but filing one took hours. We could not takeoff to fly along an airway that had another plane on it, no matter if there was altitude separation. Hotels and food were primitive in the small towns we visited and dysentery was a continuous problem. Potable water was so scarce that I authorized our pilots to fly after drinking beer when nothing else safe to drink could be found. Aircraft repair facilities were nonexistent. The Indian telephone system was so poor that I often resorted to sending a plane with a message if I was unable to complete a phone call to our dispersed aircrews.

The most useful tool for evaluating the effect of seeding was my rain rate meter. During the hectic days before departing for India, I had built a new and improved model and mounted it on the Aztec. It worked well, but the strip chart recording system was poor. It was necessary to manually count pulses on the strip chart to evaluate rainfall intensity and rainshaft size. The process was so labor intensive that we could do only cursory analyses in the field. The data was saved, but was never analyzed in depth because of the poor recording system. There were no rain gage networks or calibrated radars to use as part of an evaluation. In summary, the scientific component of Project Gromet I never really got started. The effect of our seeding, if any, will never be known.

Security of the project was eroded soon after we arrived in New Delhi. There was never any serious possibility of keeping the existence of the project secret. The Indians were not aware of the real reason for US participation, so were not highly motivated to observe tight security, even though they had promised to do so. Some of them corresponded with US scientists about the project.

Ferguson Hall, a senior State Department official, arrived one day, apparently with orders to report on how the project was doing. Pierre disliked him intensely and wanted to drive him away. Fergie wanted to ride with us on a trip to seed clouds. Pierre ordered me to put him in my plane and to deliberately scare him out of his wits! I tried to get out of it, but Pierre told me it was an order. I hedge hopped in the hot and bumpy air much of the way to Varanasi to try to make him airsick. It almost worked. After refueling, Pierre said I was to fly formation on him while he seeded clouds, so Fergie could see how it is done. I stuck to him like a shadow as he penetrated one cumulus after another, burning flares as he went. Fergie was terrified and begged me to back off. Pierre always called me the Red Baron after that. Upon our return to New Delhi, Fergie was gone in a flash. I always wondered what his trip report said and what effect it might have had on the project.

Much to Pierre's displeasure we received a message that Dr. Helmut Weickman, a NOAA scientist would be visiting to investigate what we were doing. Helmut had begun his meteorological research in Nazi Germany. After the war, he moved to the US and distinguished himself as a scientist working for the US Army. He was known for being extremely conservative, essentially an opposite of Pierre. The two men had no love for each other.

After looking around for a few days, Helmut called me aside. He said he respected me as a scientist and as one who could get things done, but he was surprised to find me working with Dr. St. Amand. It was evident that he would like to support a scientifically oriented joint US-Indian weather modification research project, but he wanted to cut Pierre St. Amand out of it. I found this degree of support, even though mixed with generous criticism of Pierre, a little surprising in view of his long held negative views on weather modification in general. I felt he was going out of his way to lend some support, even though mixed with scientific criticism. I could never judge if he had been briefed on our true purpose there. I was careful not to even hint anything about our real reason for being there to him or anyone.

With the existence of the project becoming known in the US cloud physics community, the State Department evidently felt a need to legitimize the project, and to gain scientific support for it. They organized an advisory team consisting of Dr. Roscoe Braham of the University of Chicago and Dr. Patrick Squires of the Desert Research Institute. They were among the most knowledgeable and respected scientists in the international cloud physics community. They were to study the project and make recommendations about continuation of the project, including possibly expanding it to include Pakistan. They called for me to meet with them in Washington. No other participants in the project were invited. They told me they were in a tough spot. They were aware of the importance of the project (perhaps they had been briefed on its relationship to Viet Nam), and the opportunity it represented to organize perhaps the greatest international weather modification project the world had known to that point. They told me they had serious misgivings about Pierre and his approach to weather modification. The problem, as they saw it, was to find a way for the project to move forward with scientific credibility, yet preserve the original goals. They told me I was critical to success of the project because I had the respect of the scientific community while holding the trust of Pierre and the Navy. They said they would only recommend continuation of the project if I were to direct it.

GROMET II

Negotiations for an extended Project Gromet were begun soon after we arrived in India. The Navy wanted an opportunity to work in wet tropical clouds over a long enough time to judge the effectiveness of the materials and techniques being employed. The Indians were interested in anything that would help alleviate the effects of the drought. The US proposed to fund the project from US Agency for International Development (USAID) funds, thus removing some of the effects of direct US military participation. The new Gromet II project would include several sites distributed over most of northern India, staffed jointly with Indian and US scientists. The aircraft would be provided by the US and be flown by US crews. The Indians would operate ground-based instrumentation networks and radars. Additional radars would be brought in from the US.

I was told that I would be the director of Gromet II, and was asked to work up the budget for it while at New Delhi. I was suddenly in a high pressure position that involved directing one of the largest and most complex weather modification projects conceived up to that point. Coordination of matters between scientists and cloud seeding operators from two governments would be an almost insurmountable political and technical challenge. But, I was even more worried about the absolute necessity of keeping the real reason we were there from

82

everybody while directing the project as a humanitarian and scientific effort. As a greenhorn, not yet two years out of Penn State, I was fairly certain I was getting in very much over my head in many areas.

The future of the project seemed sure enough that the Navy told me to go ahead with building seven small instrumentation systems for seeding aircraft and a complete new scientific package to replace the instrument system we installed on the Aztec for Gromet I. The plan was for the US to furnish up to 12 Cessna 210s for seeding, plus the Aztec we already had on the scene for scientific measurements. Weather Science would furnish five of the Cessna 210s, with the balance split between Tom Henderson and Lee Wilson, the two commercial cloud seeders on the job.

While wrestling with the complexities of Gromet II, I was directing the activities of Gromet I. Earlene was directing our other contract activities. We attempted to coordinate building the new instrumentation systems and our other contracts via telegram and telephone communications. Our business was barely two years old at that point, and we found ourselves unable to completely manage the flurry of issues that surfaced every day. The responsibility placed on both of us was enormous and we struggled to carry our loads.

Tom Henderson and Lee Wilson furnished most of the cloud seeding aircraft. Tom had considerable experience in international cloud seeding projects. His crew conducted themselves well, and worked well with me. Lee's people had little or no knowledge of cloud physics and even less discipline or professionalism. The idea of having to include Lee's people in cloud seeding decisions was preposterous. I was having nightmares about how I was going to balance the practical operation of that gang with the scientific expectations of the international scientific community.

Gromet I ended early in April 1967. We were to begin Gromet II in June. Pierre asked me to leave the aircraft and equipment in New Delhi for use during the summer monsoon season. At the end of Gromet I, I invited Earlene to fly to Honolulu to meet me.

We spent three days there on one of the most deserved vacations we ever had.

During that time, Weather Science was serving research projects in a half a dozen places, including Barbados, Laramie, Rapid City, Fort Collins and Fresno. Earlene had held the projects together the best she could, but numerous matters waited for me to return from India, and would wait no longer. We were building several aircraft instrumentation systems, and the customers wanted the systems finished in time for the summer cumulus season. We were growing rapidly before Project Gromet, but during the spring of 1967, we were extended well beyond our means to manage. Our children were seven and eleven years old, and at an age when we needed to spend time with them. Yet, Gromet II was an opportunity to place our little company in the forefront of meteorology on an international scale, and we knew we had to stick with it as strenuously as we could.

After a series of meetings with the Gromet II oversight committee in Washington, the State Department formed a team to negotiate with the government of India on the terms of the agreement that would govern the project. As the proposed director of Gromet II, I was a part of the team. The technical advisors were Dr. Roscoe Braham, Dr. Patrick Squires and Mr. Bob Elliott, a widely respected individual with many years of experience in weather modification operations and research.

During the negotiations in New Delhi, our teams were divided into groups of "politicians" and "technicians." After periodic general sessions, we broke into meetings with our counterparts. We were treated as very important persons in every respect, but it was clear that the Indians considered politicians superior to the technicians. My group worked out the technical details, such as the location of joint operating groups, radar installations, aircraft stations, data requirements, analysis responsibilities and organizational structure. I used one of the planes we had left at New Delhi after Gromet I to tour the sites with an Indian colleague. Some of the sites were grim. At one site in the Rajasthan Desert, we had to fuel our plane with automobile gasoline from five gallon cans hauled to the airport in a taxi. We used a shirt as a filter to avoid fuel contamination.

I was under considerable stress during this negotiation period. The project was the most exciting thing I had been able to become associated with but I was increasingly aware of the almost impossible technical, management and political challenges of the job. I knew that there were suggestions at times on the Indian side, and perhaps on our side, that I was too young to be given such a responsibility. Yet, it seemed that I was the only candidate who had the respect of the scientists from both countries and the confidence of the military brains who were behind the US funding for the project.

With the technical negotiations essentially complete, and the political discussions going well enough, I decided it was time for Earlene and the children to come to India. It looked like we would be living there, and we needed to get an idea how we would do it. Earlene got the shots, passports and visas in order.

One day, as we arrived at the Indian government building where the negotiations had been held, we got the feeling that something was wrong. The friendly VIP treatment we had accorded was suddenly correct but cool. We soon learned that the Indians had decided to break off negotiations and terminate planning for Gromet II. The reasons given had to do with economic conditions in India and shortages of scientific and technical personnel, but they were clearly not the real reasons. I was fairly sure that the Indians learned something about cloud seeding being conducted in Southeast Asia. If so, they would know that Gromet II had some major role in it – why else would the US Navy be involved. Thus, they probably felt they were unwitting allies in the development of what they saw as an evil activity. India had already taken a very negative position about US participation in the Viet Nam conflict. At any rate, the plans for the project were suddenly stopped. Pierre asked me to oversee a quick transport of all of the Gromet I equipment back to the US.

In one way, with the end of Gromet II a great weight had been lifted from my shoulders. Given the worldwide visibility and multi-national oversight of the project, it was sure to be a stressful job. With the added and undisclosed military purpose, it was a recipe for disaster. I was relieved to not have the responsibility of running it. I called Earlene to relay the news that the project we had been selected to lead no longer existed. After the family had their shots, they were certainly not glad to hear that they would not be coming to India after all.

We made arrangements to transport the Cessna aircraft, supplies and equipment via Air Force C141 transports. All personnel returned home by commercial airline. When the equipment and aircraft arrived back in the US, Project Gromet was officially finished, and our contract was terminated. We began trying to rebuild our business in the US.

Project Cloud Puff

The need for solid weather modification data to support Southeast Asia operations did not end with Gromet II. A joint Navy-Air Force-Army research project, named Cloud Puff, was formed quickly after the end of Project Gromet. It was intended to study moist cumulus clouds at selected US sites. We received another contract from the Navy to support the project.

Pierre was the Navy representative and the chief spokesman for the project. He provided the seeding materials and

With my brother, Les, and our stereo photo aircraft in New Mexico.

contractors to perform the seeding operations. Navy Lieutenant Commander Ben Livingston, who had directed early seeding operations in Southeast Asia, directed flight operations. None of the Navy crews beyond Pierre had any significant cloud physics training or experience.

Dr. Robert Cunningham, a prominent and internationally recognized cloud physics researcher, was appointed by the Air Force. He brought a very well instrumented C130 research aircraft and experienced personnel for research flight operations and data analysis to the project. Bob had serious reservations about Pierre's ideas on cloud modification, but wanted take advantage of the opportunity to study the effects of massive seeding of cumulus clouds.

The Army appointed Mr. Alex Blomerth, Director of the Atmospheric Research Laboratory at White Sands. Alex's crew had little cloud physics talent to offer the project, but they could provide logistic support. Alex and Pierre were formed an alliance that lasted for several years.

Weather Science provided several aircraft for making measurements of cloud and rain parameters at multiple levels in the clouds. We worked extensively with the Air Force crews to analyze the data collected from our aircraft.

Dr. Bob Cunningham's crew was accustomed to a very rigorous and objective approach to research, which is the norm for meteorological research. Pierre's and Alex's people were in a hurry to get results they could use to support military operations that were already in progress. These diverse approaches and requirements led to considerable discord and some hard feelings about how the experiments and analysis should be conducted. I worked hard to keep our crews on good terms with both camps.

Pierre decided we needed more rain rate measurements and cloud physics measurements than the C130 and our Aztec could do. He asked me to provide both a larger and a smaller aircraft for supplementary measurements. I bought a new Cessna 401 and a new Piper Twin Comanche. Our growing fleet then included two Piper Aztecs, a Piper Apache, a Piper Twin Comanche, a Cessna 401 and a Cessna 206. We had added four new aircraft in less than six months.

The experiments were conducted over remote areas where rain gage and radar data were scarce. By that time, I had developed a digital version of my rain rate meter and a new digital recording system. It greatly increased our efficiency in evaluating rainfall and it became the primary instrument for measuring rain volume produced by test clouds. I flew repeated passes below the cloud bases with the rain rate meter to make measurements of rain volume falling through cloud base throughout the life of the test clouds. Our other aircraft and the C130 penetrated the clouds at multiple levels to evaluate the precipitation formation processes. Large numbers of test clouds were selected, some of which were seeded and some of which were not. The selection of clouds to seed was done on a random basis. Whether the cloud was seeded or not was not revealed to the crews making the rain rate or cloud measurements or data analysis until the data analyses was complete.

We spent most of the summer of 1967 working with cumulus clouds along the Texas coast near Corpus Christi coastal clouds near Patrick Air Force Base, Florida. The program was still sorting out organizational and operational questions, so not a great deal of useful data was taken.

The tri-service project had become better organized by the summer of 1968. Alex Blomerth persuaded Bob and Pierre to bring the project to New Mexico for the summers of 1968 and 1969. Moisture from the Gulf of Mexico produces cumulus clouds over the New Mexico mountains at about the same time and place almost every day. This repeatability of similar clouds day after day was very useful for comparing the rain production of seeded and unseeded clouds. We could trace the growth of precipitation from initial precipitation formation to rain at cloud base. However, we soon became swamped in data that needed careful analysis. Our data processing was slow and labor intensive.

In order to break the data processing logjam, I purchased our first computer system, a Raytheon 16k byte, 16 bit computer with a 250k byte hard disk, a printer, a plotter and a tape drive. It cost about $100,000, about the same as the cost of the new Cessna 401. Far greater capability could be purchased today for a few hundred dollars. We mounted the system in a trailer and towed it to Alamogordo. We used it to process the data from the project aircraft overnight, so it was ready for review over breakfast. This quick turnaround data processing in the field was considered a marvelous capability for its time.

While we were supporting Cloud Puff with a large crew, we were still supporting research operations with aircrews in Rapid City, Fort Collins, Barbados and Fresno. We were still building instrumentation systems for numerous other customers. We were stretched very thin, so we used everybody, even our secretaries, on projects.

Our children lived with us in an Alamogordo motel, and even helped sometimes with posting data. The boys became as agile as water bugs in the motel pool. We watched the first landing on the Moon from our motel home in 1969.

Cloud Puff produced enough consistent data to make some assessments of the effect of seeding. Since the seeding was randomized, we were able to compare the data from seeded and unseeded clouds. The data indicated that the seeded clouds produced approximately twice the rain volume produced by the unseeded test clouds. This encouraging news gave Pierre and his crews operating in Viet Nam the basis they needed to proceed with confidence in seeding clouds to attempt to flood the Ho Chi Mihn Trail. Even though the results were encouraging, they did not answer the more important question about increasing total rainfall over a larger area. We could not refute the argument that increasing rain in the seeded clouds could have come at the expense of rainfall from nearby clouds. However, the demands of war could not wait for complete scientific results.

Fog Modification Research

Pilots in Vietnam were being shot down in large numbers. Frequently, fog prevented locating and rescuing them. There was an operational requirement for dissipating small areas of fog to make it possible to rescue pilots and perform landings at fogged-in airports.

The Navy, under Pierre St. Amand, tested a fog dissipation technique that involved spraying large volumes of ammonium nitrate-urea fertilizer into the top of the fog. If the two types of fertilizer are mixed in an equal molar ratio, the result has unusual characteristics. When mixed with water, it becomes cooler, a property known as endothermic. When mixed with 10 parts solid to one part liquid, it has approximately the viscosity of water, so high concentration droplets can be sprayed in small droplet sizes using ordinary spray nozzles. It is also extremely hygroscopic, so small droplets of the concentrate grow quickly while taking water from surrounding fog droplets. It was also relatively inexpensive and was available in bulk form in almost any agricultural community. These properties make it an ideal material for seeding warm clouds or warm fogs.

The Navy fog research project was centered at Eureka, California, one of the foggiest places in the US, especially in the winter season. The fog rolls in from the Pacific every night and often persists all day.

We furnished our Cessna 401 as a cloud physics aircraft during the winters of 1969 and 1970. China Lake contracted for a B26 to use as a spray plane. The B26 took off in the fog and made numerous passes through the fog just above the runway in attempts to clear the fog enough to land. Our Cessna 401 crew followed the B26, making measurements of fog particle sizes, liquid water content and other data. I flew the 401 part of the time and served as an advisor on cloud physics matters.

The Navy approach to fog modification produced marginal results and it was not very practical. Funding for it ended after two seasons.

Philippines

By early 1969, a protracted drought had done considerable harm to the economy of the Philippines. While it did not lead to starvation and agony as the drought in India had, it did offer another opportunity for Pierre to test his pyrotechnic devices in warm tropical clouds. Again, the project started quickly. Pierre asked me to supply instrumentation for three C130 aircraft that would be used for the seeding. By that time, we had built sixteen instrumentation systems for aircraft, and we were supporting several of them.

On this project, Pierre intended to personally conduct the seeding and have his own people do the analysis. He had had enough of meddling from Bob Cunningham, Roscoe Braham and others of the scientific community. He did not even want me involved in the science aspect of the project. I was only to supply and operate the instrumentation systems.

I had our crews remove instrumentation systems from three of our aircraft and crate them up for shipment to Clark Air Force Base. We were stretched so thin that we had no technicians to send to the Philippines to install the equipment so I decided to do it myself. I collected my tools and departed for Clark AFB. With the aid of an Air Force staff sergeant, I installed our instrumentation systems on the three C130s. I was able to get the instrumentation systems running and keep them running, so the aircraft were able to make cloud and precipitation measurements within four days after my arrival at Clark.

Pierre conducted daily briefings for the Air Force and China Lake crews. He had great admiration for military men, and they returned the respect. He did a beautiful job of explaining the theory of cloud seeding materials and how they planned to use them to modify the clouds. In my judgment, his briefings were as correct as one could make them, and they certainly motivated the crews to help him find and penetrate the target clouds.

After I had trained the China Lake crew to operate the instrumentation systems, I began riding in the cockpit to observe the seeding operation. Pierre kept up a running description of what he was observing. He pointed out the visible changes and increased growth rates that he said were due to the seeding. I considered myself to be as expert in making observations of clouds as any meteorologist in the game at that point. I quickly determined that the observed effects Pierre was pointing out and putting into the project record were, as often as not, a product of his unbounded positive attitude, but were not real.

That truth was made abundantly clear one day when Mr. Ed Yap, a high level administrator who worked for President Marcos, came along on a flight. Pierre gave Ed the VIP treatment. He pointed out in great detail the many visible changes and the dramatic growth rate increases that he told Ed were a result of seeding. The show went on for about 10 hours, during which Pierre directed about 200 flares to be fired into cumulus clouds. After we landed, I walked to the back of the aircraft to inspect the seeding racks. There, I met a panic stricken technician who blurted out that that the electrical connector for both flare racks had never been connected that day. Pierre had not fired a shot all day. Pierre later denied that it happened.

Ed Yap was the senior Philippine official appointed by President Marcos to interface with us. Ed was an interesting and controversial figure. He said he fought beside Mr. Marcos as a guerrilla during World War II. He claimed that he killed many Japanese with his 20 gauge shotgun. He had apparently stayed close to Mr. Marcos as he rose to power and, like Mr. Marcos, had become very wealthy.

There was a serious discussion going on between the Navy and the Philippine government for continuation of the seeding project on a permanent basis. I was in position to run the project. We would furnish several aircraft, and share administration responsibilities with the Philippine Weather Service. During the discussions, Ed Yap acted as the interface between the Philippine Weather Service and me. As the discussions progressed, it became very evident that I would have to pay Ed Yap some of the money I received and he would take care of the others in the government connected with the project. It was the first time I had experienced outright graft in government. I told Pierre that I couldn't deal with that kind of arrangement, declared my involvement in any future Philippine cloud seeding at an end and boarded a plane for home. Pierre then introduced Lee Wilson. Lee completed the deal and seeded clouds there for several years.

The Philippine trip was the beginning of the end of our dealings with China Lake. By refusing the Philippine project, I knew I offended Pierre. We wrapped up our reports and completed the existing contract. No further contract was offered or sought. Pierre and I remained friends over the years, even though we no longer worked together.

Senate Hearings on Weather Modification

By 1969, the security of the top secret cloud seeding project in Southeast Asia was sufficiently compromised to begin causing problems. Much of the US population was opposed to US involvement in the Southeast Asia conflict. Some politicians were looking for issues to use against the US war effort. Environmental issues were popular and politically powerful. Cloud seeding for military purposes was simultaneously an environmental and war issue that the anti-war forces could exploit.

Senator Pell called a series of hearings on the Southeast Asia cloud seeding project. The main issue was to establish that the project existed and that its purpose was to cause floods. Pierre St. Amand was one of the first to testify. A congressional staff member told me that Pierre was torn between his obligation to maintain a military secret and a contempt of Congress charge, and that he chose to deny that the project existed. Subsequent testimony by Melvin Laird, our Secretary of Defense, proved otherwise. Pierre's funding suddenly disappeared. He was finished in weather modification.

Pell Committee concluded that weather modification in any form for military purposes was repulsive and should be banned. That report led to an international treaty banning all weather modification for military purposes. The treaty ended United States military research on all aspects of weather modification. Military funding for weather modification studies, even for such things as clearing fog, soon disappeared.

Pierre and I have remained friends over the years. When I have seen him, he remembered our shared experiences with uncontained glee. Even though he did not adhere to the generally accepted procedures for scientific research, his scientific intuition was beyond any I had known. He made more of a difference in weather modification technology than most of the highly regarded members of the scientific community that tormented him so.

Air Force Geophysics Lab Experiments

Dr. Robert Cunningham and I worked together very well

during the Cloud Puff series, and we had mutual respect for the other's technical ability and ethics. We became friends as well as colleagues. I sought and finally won a series of small contracts to perform services for AFGL along the lines of what we had done for the Navy. Bob insisted that the experiments be carefully planned and executed so that the results could stand the scrutiny of the recognized cloud physicists.

Bob installed a hopper in his C130 so he could dispense several hundred pounds of ammonium nitrate-urea into the tops of warm cumulus clouds. He wanted to see if the warm cloud seeding technique could be used in lieu of silver iodide generators to seed clouds to increase rainfall in the tropics.

Bob asked me to provide one of our Aztecs with instrumentation including my rain rate meter to measure the rainfall produced by selected test clouds. The experiment was based at Patrick Air

The Cleveland Twins baseball team.

Force Base, near Cape Canaveral. Bob selected oceanic cumulus clouds that were of sufficient size to produce rain, but with tops below the freezing level so that we could be sure ice processes were not involved in rainfall production. We flew under the base of the test clouds to measure any rainfall produced. The seeding was randomized, so that only the hopper operator knew if seeding was done or not.

The experiment was conducted off the Florida coast during the summer of 1970. The success of the project there encouraged us to move the experiment to a continental location. We ran the experiment out of Tinker Air Force Base and our own facilities in Norman during the summer of 1971. The data showed a positive effect, but not significant, and not of the magnitude we saw in the oceanic cumulus off Florida.

Because our project was at home in 1971, I was able to volunteer for assistant baseball coach for our boys little league team. I had never played baseball and was utterly unqualified. They appointed me anyway, and I enjoyed the summer with my boys. We finished in the middle of the pack, and everybody seemed happy with that.

METRODATA SYSTEMS, INC.

Products for Research

Developing new instruments was as much a hobby as a business for me. I worked many hours in the shop, developing simple and reliable means of recording the basic variables and packaging them in standard size modules. These standardized modules enabled us to assemble airborne meteorological data systems quickly, and to change the configuration according to the needs of a particular project.

As the reputation of these systems grew, we received orders for the instrumentation modules from research projects around the world. By 1967, our commercial products sales were growing rapidly. I formed a new company, Metrodata Systems, Inc. for the purpose of producing and selling data collection systems, leaving Weather Science, Inc. to concentrate on atmospheric research and services.

The rain rate meter continued to be my pet project. Rain droplet spectra and water content were considered to be two of the most important variables in evaluating any cloud physics experiment, especially weather modification experiments. The rain rate meter was the first instrument developed that could give a voltage pulse proportional to the mass of each raindrop encountered. The rain rate meter became a standard instrument for cloud physics studies as far away as South Africa.

DL-620

The available means of recording the data in aircraft were very crude. Light beam oscillographs were commonly used for recording analog data. We instrumented twenty civilian aircraft and five C130 transports, using light beam oscillographs. The process of extracting information from so many strip charts was very labor intensive, not very accurate and prone to errors.

I recognized as early as 1962 that we needed a digital data acquisition system to record our data on magnetic tape. Such

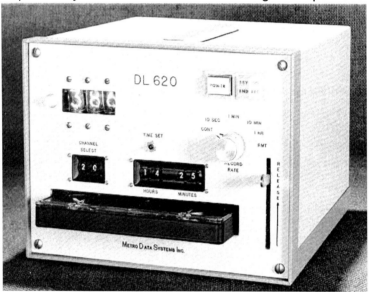

The DL620 digital data acquisition system enabled computer processing of research data.

systems were just being introduced at that time. However, they were large, very expensive, required lots of power and did not seem practical for use in small aircraft. I wanted to develop a simple, lightweight digital data acquisition system. Our chief engineer, Bob Cook, and I began development of an analog to digital converter, multiplexer and crystal-controlled clock. These were the main elements of a new digital data acquisition system.

We packaged these systems and an endless loop magnetic tape deck in a 2/3 cubic foot aluminum box. We designed a companion unit that could read the tapes into any of the minicomputers that were becoming common in research community. We named the new product the DL-620. We could make it for about $1700. We decided to sell it for $4200, which was a fraction of the price of its nearest competitor.

I felt that we had finally come up with a product that had a broad market and we were well ahead of the competition. I knew leads in the electronics business are short lived, and if we were to exploit our new product, we would need to move swiftly. I began developing a network of sales representatives for the United states and selected foreign markets.

By late 1969, Metrodata was making a strong showing in the electronics manufacturing business and it appeared that the company could make a transition from a scientific organization to an electronics manufacturer. We were attracting attention from investment bankers and potential investors who thought the company would be a good candidate for going public within a year or two. I began reading everything I could find on the subject of finding investors and going public.

Gould, Inc. Contract

In early 1970, I received a call from Don Nicksay, the president of the Brush Recorder Division of Gould, Inc. Brush recorders had long been the industry standard for accurate, reliable and robust strip chart recorders. Incredibly, the company had invested almost nothing in developing new recording technologies. Somebody at Brush apparently woke up to the fact that electronic data recording was a rapidly growing new market, and they had nothing under development.

Don Nicksay visited us to look over the DL620 product. After having his engineers assess the technology we had developed, he announced that he wanted to buy Metrodata. He gave signals that he was willing to offer a price of somewhere around $1 Million for the company, a very large sum in those days.

Earlene and I briefly discussed the potential sale. We had come to feel very close to the company and its people. We knew that the company would be moved to Cleveland, Ohio and be absorbed into the big Brush monolith. It seemed that we would be killing something that had become a second family to us. We knew that we had a good product line and it was selling well. I told Don Nicksay we could not sell.

He then offered to buy the digital data product line. When we again refused to sell, he offered to sign an exclusive marketing agreement to sell our data recording products under the Brush name. We would be required to drop our sales representative organization, which had just begun to work effectively, and sell our digital products through Brush. In return, they would guarantee us a minimum buy of 200 DL-620s the next year, with promises of increased buys in future years. Brush would also adopt the new designs we were working on under the same arrangement.

This deal offered us a relatively certain $200,000 profit on the DL-620 line the first year and sharply increasing profits in future years. It would not prevent us from developing products outside the digital recorder line and marketing them directly to our customers. It seemed like a certain road to success, so we accepted.

Brush soon had a contract in our hands. After a short period of negotiations, we signed the contract. It was to be one of our life lessons.

Winding Down

By 1970, I believed we would need additional space for manufacturing. I bought a 6 acre site for a new building about 1/4 mile from of Westheimer Field. The 10,000 square foot building was finished in March 1971 at a cost of $172,000, including the land and improvements.

By late 1970, our first order of 50 DL-620 units had been completed and Brush was dragging its feet on the scheduled follow-on orders. When we pressed them on their obligation to buy DL-620 units, they made excuses about the product not meeting Brush standards or not suited to their markets. I learned that Brush was courting key members of our staff, obviously to develop their own competing line of products. Hoyt Hart, one of our key employees, did join the Gould team.

I consulted an attorney in Oklahoma City and Sam Whitlock, our own attorney in Norman, about the Gould problem. Both advised me that we had good grounds to sue Gould for recovery of our product and damages, but that we would be up against a giant with very deep pockets, and that they would be able to string us along for years. It looked like we would be broke long before we could recover anything from Gould. We finally elected to go for a cancellation of the contract by mutual consent to get our product back.

Gould still had most of the first fifty DL-620 units they bought from us on the shelf, so they started selling them at fire sale prices, undermining our own sales. They had effectively killed our most profitable product and cost us dearly.

We quickly turned to developing new products that were better suited to the developing Environmental Protection Agency environmental monitoring requirements. The investment in developing and marketing these new products exhausted our cash reserves and led to cash flow problems. I began liquidating our fleet of aircraft to raise cash.

By 1972, cash flow was a serious problem. Weather Science was no longer generating cash from the weather modification projects, and was bidding on low percentage projects that were not in its main strength. The DL-620 was a four year old design and had serious competition by more modern designs. Our credit was no longer solid. Vendors increasingly insisted on shipping to us COD. We were having difficulty recreating the sales representative network that we had abandoned with the signing of the Gould contract.

We discovered that an employee had embezzled over $4,000. Our comptroller, had other interests than monitoring the business of the company and had let our business office become chaotic. One day, he wrote himself two large checks to which he was not entitled and walked out.

Earlene resumed control over the business office. She and

Linda Parrish began to reorganize and revitalize the business office.

By mid 1973, our financial status was critical. Our ability to ship products and the quality of those products was suffering. I sold our building for $300,000 and leased it back, generating almost $150,000 in cash. I invested most of that in development of the DL640, a new data recording technology that could compete in new markets.

The development and introduction of the new DL-640 product took longer and cost more to develop than we had estimated. By mid 1974, we were again in a severe cash flow bind just as the new DL-640 product line was beginning to sell.

I found two investors from California, Art Steele and Al Block, who were interested in our data system technology for oil well logging applications. We negotiated a deal whereby they would take our stock and assume our debt. Earlene and I received no money for our stock. It was a bitter experience to walk away from ten years of intense effort with nothing at all to show for it. However, we were out from under the strain and crises of the past few years and it felt good.

Art and Al marketed our products for down-hole data recording and advertised heavily in the rapidly expanding oil exploration business. They were successful in expanding sales in the new market and sold the company for a good profit about two years later.

NEW START

New Company

We formed Aeromet, Inc. in August of 1974, just after I left Metrodata. I converted our garage into an office/shop for me. We set up a business office for Earlene in our living room. We had started Weather Science that same way ten years earlier. This time, we told ourselves, it will not end the same way.

We won a small contract with the Environmental Protection Agency. They needed a climatological database for wind and temperature up to 2000 feet for several sites in the western US where major power plants were planned.

I proposed to collect wind and temperature data by using a small temperature-measuring sonde to be carried on a balloon and tracked by a theodolite. I enlisted the help of a consultant to help redesign our old transponder from our tornado research days and the companion receiver. I called it the T-Sonde system. I hired a custom manufacturer to manufacture the thousands of T-Sondes we would need. This subcontracting arrangement worked so well I wondered why I had put up with the manufacturing problems at Metrodata.

We had no regular employees. Earlene handled the books and contract matters. I handled the technical problems. Larry and Garry converted the upstairs recreation room to a parachute factory and made several thousand small parachutes for the T-Sondes. The boys and I flew in our Twin Comanche to the field sites to install the equipment. We hired

I broke this beautiful appaloosa to ride. Here, I was riding him in a parade.

and trained operators at each site. Karen helped supply helium, balloons and T-Sondes to the sites. It was truly a family business, and we had fun with it.

One day, Earlene noticed that the Hanksville, Utah, site was using far more helium and balloons than the other sites. We asked the operator there why she was using so much helium. She said there were too many cats in town, so she started catching them, tying them onto a balloon and launching them.

We were horrified at the thought of those poor frozen cats falling from the sky. We told her to find a more humane way to get rid of the cats.

Keep It Small, Smell the Roses

During our years at Penn State and the 10-year run with Weather Science and Metrodata, I worked long hours every day. During those years, our family time was often too short and too scattered. As we phased out of Metrodata/Weather Science, we promised ourselves that we would keep our business small for a few years so we could spend time with our children, who were at an age when it was important for us to do so.

Mom and Dad lived on the edge of Grand Lake during those years. Dad liked to fish and raise an extensive garden and orchard. It was a golden time for them. We bought a sailboat and left it at the lake. The boys and I loved to sail when the wind was strong and there were no other boats on the lake. The girls didn't care for that kind of sailing, but found plenty of fun around the lake anyway. We were able to spend many weekends at the lake and it was good for the family.

Earl and Martha Hobbs had a prosperous ranch near Haskell. They thought all of their grandchildren were the best in the world. They loved it when we came to the farm for a weekend, which was often. There were horses to ride, cattle to drive and good fishing in our choice of farm ponds. During the years when the company was small, we spent most weekends either at Grand Lake or on the Hobbs farm.

Africa

Merlin Williams, an old friend from weather modification days, called in September 1974. He was acting as a consultant for Ambassador Andre Salifou, of Niger, West Africa. A prolonged drought had devastated the economy of Niger to the point that most of the animal population was dead or dying and people were dying of hunger. Ambassador Salifou believed that a cloud seeder could bring the rain they needed. Merlin asked if I would submit a bid for providing cloud seeding services in Niger, beginning the following week.

Merlin knew that I didn't like promising things that cloud seeding cannot deliver. We both knew that a time of drought is a bad time to begin cloud seeding because conditions for seeding are generally poor and the sponsors usually expect a miracle. Merlin said he was telling the ambassador all of those things but he wanted me to submit a bid anyway. I computed a price for an emergency cloud seeding effort that evening and submitted it early the following morning.

Before noon, Merlin called to say I was hired, and that I should have planes and seeding equipment in Niger the following Wednesday, ready to begin seeding. Once again, I was asked to deliver aircraft and equipment on an almost impossible schedule.

I leased two Twin Comanche's that I had used previously for cloud seeding and installed ferry tanks. By drawing on favors here and there, I was able to have everything ready to ship by the following Wednesday.

There were no questions asked when I checked the cloud seeding materials, which were class C explosives, as excess baggage to take with me.. However, upon arrival at Dakar, Senegal a customs agent found them. I knew I was in trouble. The customs people spoke no English and I could speak only a few words of French. I was in danger of having my seeding materials confiscated, even if they didn't throw me in jail. I called Ambassador Salifou in Washington. He arranged for a Nigerian student from a nearby university to come to the airport and act as an interpreter. After considerable intense discussion, the young man told me that if I could come up with $250 in cash for the customs men, everything would be all right. That was the only bribe I ever paid.

A French crew flew a military C47 to Dakar to deliver my materials and me to Niamey, the capital of Niger. The Twin Comanches arrived about the same time. The Niger government provided very nice accommodations for us in buildings that were built by NASA for spacecraft communications in the early Mercury Space Program days.

As luck would have it, moisture arrived over Niger just after we did. We found what appeared to be favorable cloud conditions and we seeded everything we could find. The rains began. The Niger government praised us for bringing the blessed rain. I tried to tell them that Mother Nature had turned a corner, and that we had little or nothing to do with it, but I could tell they weren't listening. They gave us the credit for the rain anyway. That was one of the problems I always had with cloud seeding – people expect it to perform miracles and it cannot.

I told the government that I would help set up a team using their own meteorologists and pilots to do their own cloud seeding, but did not want to continue seeding myself. They liked the idea. The ambassador contracted with me to provide two seeding aircraft, equipment and materials for both cold cloud and warm cloud seeding. I provided them with two new weather radars for the airports at Niamey and Zinder. I modified the radars so they could display aircraft transponder signals in the control towers as well as their normal weather radar function. Those were the first radars ever installed in Niger. The two aircraft were the 15th and 16th aircraft registered in the history of the country. It was a primitive country.

Consulting Business

I was hired by the State of South Dakota to inspect operation of their cloud seeding contractors in the summer of 1975. Since I would be traveling most of the time, we bought a used motor home so the whole family could travel with me. The boys, Renee, Earlene and I had one of the most pleasant summers ever. Karen elected to stay in Norman where she could be with her friends.

I began receiving calls to serve as an expert witness in court cases where weather had played a part in aircraft accidents. My job was to provide expert testimony about what part weather might have played in causing the accident. I studied the weather data, pilot's radio transmissions, FAA flight track data, the condition of the wreckage and anything I could find that had any bearing on the case. My testimony in court seemed to influence the decisions of the juries. Because of my experience in heavy-weather flying, lawyers began asking me to testify on pilot factors in addition to weather factors.

I enjoyed the challenge of reconstructing the factors involved in accidents. I also liked the challenge of doing battle with lawyers in the courtroom. I knew my subject well and stayed with the facts so it was easy to defend myself against snarling lawyers.

I began using other meteorologists to assist in collecting the weather data and performing routine analyses. However, the lawyers insisted that I appear personally for court testimony. I was at the mercy of the court appearance schedules. I eventually had to end the consulting business as our project business began growing again. I had 26 cases open when I decided I had to shut down the consulting business.

Contractor Again

In October 1975, I heard about an Air Force Geophysics Laboratory request for proposals (RFP) that sounded like something we should bid on. The project, called the Reentry Environment Measurements Program (REMP), involved making cloud measurements using an instrumented Learjet to support missile re-entry tests at Kwajalein, Marshall Islands and Wallops Island, Virginia.

I called my old friend Bob Cunningham at AFGL to ask what was going on. He told me the RFP had been out about six weeks and proposals were due in four days. He said that Meteorology Research, Inc., the incumbent contractor, was building the instrumentation system and was to install it on the Learjet. MRI had leased the Learjet and would operate it, no matter who won the instrumentation contract. MRI was an old and well established meteorological services company whose reputation had suffered some since Paul MacCready, its founder, had left it a few years before.

The odds against winning the contract were astronomical. MRI and at least one other bidder had been working on their proposals for months and I had not even seen the RFP. I was not familiar with many of the instrument systems MRI was proposing to use. I had no staff, no facility and no tools. Our office consisted of my desk and workbench in the converted garage and Earlene's desk in our living room.

I called Joe Candura, the contracting officer at AFGL, and asked him to send a copy of the RFP by Federal Express. When it came, we had only two days to write and mail our proposal. The RFP was very confusing. We learned later that some vital pages had been omitted from the copy Joe sent to us. So, in addition to the other long odds, I was dealing with an incomplete RFP.

We decided to send a proposal in spite of the obvious futility of doing so. We worked the next two days with less than four hours of sleep. I contacted a few individuals that promised to join us if we were to win. However, none of them had any experience with the hardware or software we were proposing to use. I wrote resumes for them that sounded as good as possible without stretching the truth too much. I wrote a technical and cost proposal and Earlene typed the whole thing. I did a budget estimate based mostly on guesses since I had no time to obtain real cost data. We delivered the proposal to Federal Express at the last minute. We collapsed and slept for a whole day.

A few days later, I received a call from Don McLeod, a meteorologist on Bob Cunningham's staff. He indicated that AFGL would send a team to perform a site survey. I invited him to come, even though I knew we had nothing for them to survey. About a week later, Don, an engineer and a technician showed up at our door for the site visit. We poured them a cup of coffee and sat around our dining table to talk since there was nothing for them to see. We talked about the good old days when we were doing the Cloud Puff experiments. We were embarrassed at having them come for a site survey with nothing to see. I could see that they were embarrassed for us.

Joe Candura scheduled a site visit at the MRI facility so the bidders could see the Learjet and the instrumentation system that MRI was installing. I asked Bill Myers, our proposed engineer, to join me there. MRI avoided giving any useful information about their instrumentation system. I could see that it was surprisingly crude and poorly designed. Bill and I agreed that the system probably would never work, even in the hands of the people who designed it.

Joe Candura scheduled a proposal review in Los Angeles. I had no staff, so I went to the meeting alone. The panel, consisting of Joe Candura and six technical experts from AFGL, asked me all sorts of complex questions about cloud physics, radar, computer processing and engineering. At the end, Joe Candura turned to my cost estimate. He asked about the meaning of the words "WAG" or "SWAG" in the column labeled "Basis of Estimate". I knew I was in deep trouble, but answered truthfully that it meant "Wild Ass Guess" or "Scientific Wild Ass Guess", depending on whether I had any information at all about the cost. He leaned back and laughed so hard his big belly shook like Jell-O. He declared that I had to be the most truthful contractor he had ever interviewed.

Joe Candura called one morning with the news that we had been

The REMP team documented the types and concentrations of cloud particles and water content encountered by reentering test vehicles. Here multiple warheads are seen in time lapse hitting their targets.

selected for the contract! I knew that AFGL's technical people must have given us the nod based on what I had done for them in the past – it certainly was not based on our current capabilities. They took a tremendous leap of faith in awarding us the contract. If we failed, it would have reflected badly on their careers. MRI took the loss very badly and I knew they would do everything they could to make us fail.

When I arrived at Ontario Airport to take possession of the instrumentation system and move the Learjet to Norman, MRI said that the system was at least three weeks from being finished and the Air Force would just have to wait for them to finish it. An Air Force representative called me aside, expressed his irritation at MRI and asked if I thought I could complete the system in time to make the first mission. Even though I had no engineer, no shop, no tools and almost no idea how the stuff was supposed to work, I told him I thought I could get there with enough of it working to support the mission.

I had the Learjet crew deliver the aircraft to Catlin Aviation in Oklahoma City. I assembled every technician and engineer I knew who was willing to work on the system, essentially around the clock. We tore out the huge studio-style intercom and voice recording systems and installed a new one designed for use in aircraft. The computer program crashed frequently but it seemed to compute cloud water content reasonably well. The particle measuring probes worked, but calibration was a problem. Two major instruments, called a Formvar replicator and a Total Water Content Meter were in hopeless disarray. I decided to do the first mission without them. I sent Harold Bowles, a technician and Phil Stickel, a meteorologist to Particle Measuring Systems, Inc. in Boulder for a special school on the theory and practice of operating and maintaining the PMS probes.

After several extremely long days, we flew the Learjet to Wallops Island for the first mission. To the amazement and heartfelt relief of the Air Force people, we managed to collect useful cloud particle data in support of the mission. While our liquid water content computations were a bit crude, they served the immediate need. MRI still retained the contract to provide the

Learjet. Their representative was hostile and uncooperative. I resolved to take that contract from MRI at the first opportunity.

I worked long hours to understand how the systems were supposed to work and to train the personnel I had hired quickly after the contract award. We had our first mission at Kwajalein in early February, about two months after we took over the aircraft. It was fairly successful. We continued supporting missions at Kwajalein and at Wallops Island and our data product improved. I replaced the unworkable instrument systems as rapidly as I could with smaller and more reliable systems. I had outstanding support from the Air Force Geophysics Lab personnel. They were wonderful people to deal with, and as professional as any I met during my career.

The REMP contract was rebid in 1977 with the added task of providing the Learjet and its crew. We beat MRI again. We retained the same basic contract through numerous rebids over twenty-five years. During that time, the contract value grew from the initial $125,000 per year to over $15 million per year. I began flying as copilot on the Learjet. I achieved an airline transport rating and became type rated in the Learjet in 1979. I began flying as captain on all missions because I could better observe clouds and direct the mission from the cockpit.

Our customers were pleased with our performance under the REMP contract. We were asked to suggest improvements for the instrumentation system. We eventually replaced all of the systems that MRI had installed with newer, smaller, and much more effective systems. We installed a very advanced REMP control system in the weather station that could download telemetry data from the aircraft and from the range radars. We were able to quickly and efficiently assess and forecast missile reentry conditions, thus saving standby costs on ranges from Vandenberg to Kwajalein. By 1980, the REMP project was running smoothly.

Move to Tulsa

One evening in 1977, while flying back to Oklahoma City from a business trip, I looked down on Tulsa and began thinking about a move to Tulsa. Earlene had always wanted to live there.

Most of our business suppliers were located in Tulsa. There were more engineers in the labor pool in Tulsa than in Oklahoma City. Tulsa would be two hours closer to Grand Lake and Earl and Martha's farm, where we spent many weekends. I decided that, while our company only employed a half dozen people, it would be feasible to make the move. I knew we would build another company, and then it would be too difficult to move.

We found a house about 10 miles southeast of downtown Tulsa, but it needed considerable work. We moved in late 1977. The boys and I painted the house, landscaped the yard, built a large redwood deck, installed a pool, built a redwood fence and installed an automatic sprinkler system.

We were unable to find a suitable office for our business. There were no suitable hangars or offices at the airport as there had been in Norman. We rented a small building on 47th Place, near Mingo, about 20 minutes from the airport. The building was in a poor location and ill-suited to our needs. Work on aircraft required many time-consuming trips to the airport. I continued searching for a better business location.

Karen was attending the University of Oklahoma and living in a sorority house. We arranged to have the boys attend Broken Arrow High School where the advanced courses the boys wanted were available. They graduated at the top of their class. They lived at home while they earned their BS degrees at the University of Tulsa. They became expert computer programmers and contributed to Aeromet's software development efforts. Renee adapted easily to Union and later Jenks schools. Karen and Tim Cline were married at our home in December 1978.

Another Downturn

One of President Carter's last acts was to drastically cut the budget of the Air Force Ballistic Missiles Office, our major customer. BMO had to cancel or delay the tests scheduled for 1981 and the 1982 schedule looked doubtful. In order to cut costs, BMO asked us to demodify the Learjet and place the instrument systems in storage. We had to lay off most of team we had developed for the REMP contract. Our company was suddenly on hard times again.

The hoped-for BMO mission requirements did not develop for 1982. We realized that BMO would be years in rebuilding their test requirements to the point they would need us again. We continued to struggle with minor contracts for the next three years. We were forced to lay off most of our employees. We were so discouraged with the boom and bust cycles in defense programs that we seriously considered getting out of government contracting altogether.

Earlene cut her finger one day in early 1980 and it would not stop bleeding. We consulted a hematologist, Dr. Robert Cossman. He found that her platelet count was very low. After months of extensive testing, it was determined that her spleen was the cause of her problem and that it must be removed. It was a major operation and we were very concerned. She came through the operation well and recovered slowly in the following months.

BUILDING ANOTHER COMPANY

Reagan Defense Buildup

In 1980, President Reagan campaigned on, among other things, a strong defense. Upon being elected, he began developing plans to rebuild America's military strength. I knew the new weapon systems being started would eventually need field tests and would provide new opportunities for us. I looked for opportunities to develop systems that we could use when we resumed airborne field test support.

Airborne Cloud Characterization Radar (ACCR)

Earlene and I attended a two week conference on radar and cloud physics in Clairmont Ferrand, France. It was a chance for us to get away for a couple of weeks and tour a part of the world we had never seen. Between sessions, we explored the sights around central France.

My imagination was fired up by a paper on K_a band radar. I began developing a plan in my mind to build a K_a band (8 mm wavelength) for characterizing the atmosphere in the reentry corridor at Kwajalein. Because of its extremely short wavelength, a K_a band radar can detect cloud particles that are much too small to be detected by other more normal radars. My plan was to mount it on an aircraft so it would look vertically downward and detect the thin clouds below the aircraft. My mind became so involved with the radar that I could think of little else during the conference.

Upon returning home, I contacted BMO for an appointment to propose developing the radar, which I called the Airborne Cloud Characterization Radar (ACCR). My proposal was accepted with little delay and was funded at an adequate level.

I began development of the radar in 1981. I had considerable experience with X (3 cm wavelength) and S band (10 cm wavelength) radars, but I had much to learn about the extremely difficult K_a (8 mm) wavelength band. I hired two consultants who had K_a band experience, Dr. Roger Lhermitte and Dr. Fausto Pasqualucci, to guide the design. I also hired Terry Gerdes, an electrical engineer and Nathan Funk, a meteorologist-engineer who had done his MS thesis on a K_a band ground-based radar. We built a very sophisticated radar with what was called polarization diversity and Doppler capability. In addition to sensing reflected energy from very small cloud and precipitation particles, we could determine whether the particles were made of liquid water or ice. The Doppler capability enabled us to measure the vertical velocity of the particles. No airborne radar up to that time had achieved such a capability. It was considered to be advanced technology at that time. Even though the sophisticated features proved difficult to maintain and were later phased out, the ACCR proved to be extremely valuable for reentry environment requirements. It was a vital tool for cloud experiments for many years.

A New Home Base

By late 1982, I could see developing opportunities in defense contracting. I felt there was a chance for us to again develop a company based on airborne measurements and technology.

Yet, our business was stuck in a poorly designed building that was not near any airport. We needed a new home on an airport. I found a large hangar facility for sale at Riverside Airport. It was occupied by a very poorly run fixed base operation (FBO).

A decision to buy the building involved a great deal of risk. We would have to borrow the total price at a the then-prevailing very high interest rate. The building was much larger than we needed and would be a heavy overhead burden that could sink the company. I decided to take the risk and bought the building. Fortunately, we were able to win additional contracts, so the gamble paid off. We added a new office section in 1986 and a major expansion of the hangar and office space in 1990. Our business expanded rapidly in the 1980s so we bought an additional hangar/office building on the north end of the airport in 1989.

Aircraft Launched Atmospheric Sounding System (ALMET)

Missile tests are generally conducted over oceans far from any land for safety reasons. Most of those tests require detailed measurements of atmospheric temperature and wind profiles up to about 100,000 feet altitude. The Navy Trident

After being dropped from an aircraft the ALMET inflated a weather balloon during descent, then release the balloon and radio-sonde just before hitting the water.

Office needed a better way to get the soundings. I suggested an atmospheric sounding that could be launched from an aircraft that would be in the target area anyway. They were skeptical because they had spent $3 million trying to develop such a device with no success.

I had developed a concept for such a device during my Penn State days. I worked with two engineers to construct a prototype using my Penn State concept. We launched two of them from a Caribou cargo plane at Kwajalein. Both worked well enough to persuade the Navy to fund further development, leading to a production model that the Navy still uses. We called it the aircraft-launched meteorological sounding system, ALMET for short. It is normally launched from a Navy P3 submarine hunter aircraft. The package descends to the ocean on a parachute. A balloon is inflated atop the parachute during the descent. At 50 feet above the water, the balloon and sonde are released. The sonde then transmits temperature, humidity and wind information as it rises from sea level to about 80,000 to 100,000 feet altitude. To my knowledge, it is the only such device ever developed and produced.

Autonomous Unmanned Reconnaissance Aircraft (AURA)

With the Figure prospect of increased missile tests under the Reagan defense buildup, I could see a need for an unmanned aircraft that could fly in the reentry corridor during reentry to take meteorological and optical data. Manned aircraft required to keep a safe distance during the critical reentry phase.

In 1982, I proposed to develop an autonomous unmanned reconnaissance aircraft (AURA) to fly in the reentry corridor when manned aircraft could not. I proposed to use an existing airframe design with a modified commercial autopilot and a microprocessor control system that could fly a mission completely autonomously. Vic Puckett, our Army contract technical monitor, liked the idea.

The AURA in autonomous flight mode.

I decided to base the AURA on an experimental canard design called the Rutan Long Ez. With its rear-mounted engine and stall-proof design, it was an ideal platform for meteorological and optical sensors. I bought a Long Ez for the project.

Our first task was to develop a computer-controlled autopilot that could fly an entire pre-programmed mission with no human intervention. We selected S-Tec, an upstart autopilot manufacturer who had already developed a computer interface for its autopilot. We developed a microprocessor system that could be programmed for a mission and output the required controls for the autopilot. That phase of the project was accomplished fairly easily.

The more difficult task was to make the autopilot land the aircraft with minimal or no inputs from a remote pilot. We developed a hand-held command box that enabled a remote pilot to send correction signals to the autopilot, while keeping the autopilot in control of the aircraft down to touchdown on the runway.

Upon receiving an enable command, the autoland system controlled airspeed to a pre-set value, usually 90 knots. Then, the system would intercept a localizer and glide slope for an automated approach to the runway. At 100 feet altitude, the system began using radar altimeter data to flare the aircraft and cut the throttle. Upon touchdown, it used signals from a turn rate gyro to apply differential braking to keep the aircraft going straight down the runway. The system was successful except that the autopilot was sloppy in pitch axis control and we were never able to fully correct the problem. The S-Tec autopilot turned out to be a poor choice in our design.

The intended operational payload would need a larger payload capability than the Long Ez could provide. Ken Winter and I developed a prototype aircraft that was similar to the Long Ez but with a cockpit twice as wide as the Long Ez. The cockpit would have accommodated four seats, had we elected to put seats in it. It was designed with conventional spars and ribs made of fiberglass. We developed tooling that could be used to produce interchangeable parts so the aircraft could be produced in quantity.

I was very interested in the AURA project so I supervised every aspect of the design from concept through detailed fabrication. The aircraft that evolved was beautiful. Its sleek lines suggested its low drag and sturdy construction. Its sophisticated computerized control system was capable of almost complete autonomy on takeoff and landing and could execute complex flight plans with complete autonomy. The computer could monitor the health of the aircraft and make a number of decisions on its own. Under certain conditions, such as loss of the electrical generator, the AURA could automatically abort the mission and return home on battery power.

I flew as the "guinea pilot" on almost all of the development flights. My job was to maintain contact with Air Traffic Control and watch for other aircraft while monitoring the performance of the AURA while it was under computer control. I could take manual control if needed, but that was usually not necessary.

Even though we had some government funding, Aeromet funded

most of the development of the AURA. By the time we finished the AURA, the mission of the Kwajalein Missile Range had changed and an unmanned aircraft was no longer needed. The Army signed over all rights to the AURA to Aeromet.

Shortly thereafter, there was a period of concern in the US because Iran had become very belligerent and had deployed Silkworm missiles along its shoreline to threaten US Navy ships in the Persian Gulf. Army Colonel Ward Lutz who was responsible for Army remotely piloted aircraft programs decided the AURA was just what the Army needed for reconnaissance over the sites and was preparing an order for four aircraft. At Col. Lutz's urging, we began production of four aircraft while he processed an order for them. The order never came because the threat suddenly went away. We were left with an investment in parts and a second aircraft with no place to sell them.

During Desert Storm, we were asked to fly a series of low level research flights at night time over a desert test range in Arizona. Ken Winter was eager to make the flights. The tests went well until Ken descended to an unsafe altitude for some reason. Unfortunately, he clipped the crest of a hill. The aircraft was destroyed and Ken was killed. Ken's father came to the site and made arrangements to have his body cremated. We were all devastated. Ken was a hard working, dedicated and likeable engineer and aviator. That accident had much to do with my next decision.

During this same period, Aeromet had become very successful with airborne optical measurement systems. I had to make a decision as to whether to put our major emphasis on the airborne optical sensors or the AURA. The market looked much safer and larger for the airborne optical systems. I made the decision to ground the AURA. I donated the second prototype to the Tulsa Air and Space Museum. It will remain there on permanent display as an inspiration to youngsters interested in aviation.

I regard the AURA as one of the most significant technical achievements of my career. However, it was a failure from the business standpoint. It is now a bitter-sweet memory.

The Homing Overlay Experiment (HOE)

By 1982, I could see that the several new programs that were being started as part of President Reagan's defense buildup would lead to field tests and a need for the kind of services we could provide.

I found an opportunity in a new Army program, called the Homing Overlay Experiment. Its purpose was to develop the first missile that could intercept and kill a target reentry vehicle. This required that the interceptor be guided to within a few inches of the center of a target that would be moving at a speed about 16,000 miles per hour. The feat was compared to shooting a falling dime at 20 miles range. It was essential that any successful HOE intercept be well documented.

The HOE program office wanted to use airborne cameras to

The Conquest with twelve cameras for recording missile intercepts.

document the planned intercept. I asked for an opportunity to bid for the job. After dragging its feet until the very last minute, the Army awarded us a contract to develop the airborne camera systems needed to document the intercept.

I found Wally Boquist of Bedford, Massachusetts who was willing and able to take the photographic part of the job. Wally had made a career of photographing military experiments, especially those requiring very fast or sensitive cameras. He was well qualified and had the required equipment. He proved to be a very talented but temperamental co-contractor.

The aircraft was a problem. Wally thought we needed a jet, but the program could not afford one. I proposed a Conquest II, a high performance corporate turboprop with a large cabin and large windows. Unable to finance a Conquest II, I was forced to lease the only one I could find available under a lease. I installed a pair of Omega navigation systems and a dual HF communications system to enable us to navigate over the ocean. The whole system was crude and not very reliable, but it met the bare minimum requirements of the project. I certainly wasn't proud of it.

The unreliability of the Conquest and its systems made the ferry flights difficult and dangerous. On one trip, I discovered that the left main tire was flat upon landing at Ontario, California. I had a new one installed. Inexplicably, the new tire was flat when I landed in Seattle. I spent a day having the wheel X-rayed, a new O ring and a new tire installed just to be sure that nothing further could go wrong. I reached Cold Bay, Alaska, late at night and in the midst of a raging blizzard. I made a very turbulent and difficult approach to landing. As the left main gear touched, my heart sank - the tire was flat again! I fixed the problem the next day by installing a tube from another aircraft tire.

The Conquest had a way of breaking down at critical times. Once, the directional gyro failed after the target missile had been launched. Without heading information, the Omega/VLF navigation systems would be hopelessly lost in a few minutes. We were 300 miles from the nearest island. I managed to save the mission by manually keying in heading readings from the wet compass while flying the aircraft by hand and operating my computer to determine when   to make the required turns to be on station as the target reentered the atmosphere. We were on station and got good pictures. The HOE people never knew we were hanging on by our fingernails to get the photographic data, then get back home safely.

In spite of several similar breakdowns at critical times, I always found ways to have the aircraft on station and the cameras aimed at the intended intercept point for each of four missions. The first three interceptors missed their mark, but the fourth was a smashing (literally) success. Our pictures, video and movie film were used extensively by the Reagan administration in selling the Congress on funding for the Strategic Defense Initiative ("Starwars").

Even though the HOE Project was difficult and troublesome, it paved the way for us to win larger and much more important contracts as the Reagan defense buildup continued to grow.

Kwajalein Weather Station

In 1983, Vic Puckett, our contract technical monitor, asked if we would be interested in bidding for a contract to operate the weather station at Kwajalein. I jumped at the chance. On my word that we would bid it, the Army issued a request for proposals that was set aside for small businesses only.

By that time, I had a great deal of experience in tropical meteorology. I was familiar with the shortcomings and needs of the weather station, so I was able to write a very strong proposal to operate the weather station. We won the competition easily.

In our proposal, I promised the Army that I would dramatically improve the products and services of the weather station through modernization, higher quality personnel and much better management. However, that was a time of heavy budget pressure, so no improvement and modernization funds were available.

I was determined to find ways to save enough money in the operating budget to pay for some of the needed improvements. We hired young meteorologists with recent MS degrees as forecasters, replacing the retired enlisted forecasters. Even though they were relatively new to tropical forecasting, they were experts in use of computers. We introduced the first computers into the weather station at our own expense. We trained the forecasters to make the weather observations that had previously required a staff of observers. They money we saved was used to buy a network of VAX computers. We motivated the forecasters to develop software to process incoming data and produce displays in addition to their regular duties. When the computers and software were in place we threw the teletypes and fax machines into the sea. Range customers were impressed with the improvements in weather station and its products.

After the success of the first round of improvements, it was easier to obtain funds for modernization. I hired Lynn Rose, an

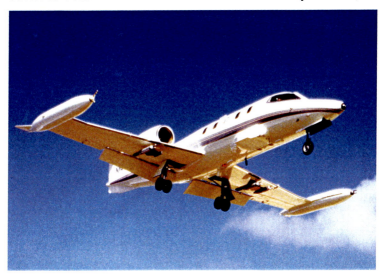

The REMP Learjet was heavily instrumented with cloud particle probes under the wings and in the tip tanks, a down-looking radar under the fuselage and an up-looking laser radar on top of the fuselage.

MS meteorology graduate of the University of Oklahoma, to run the weather station and other meteorological functions of Aeromet.   We   were   able   to   obtain   funds   for   further improvements. We installed a new satellite data handling system, a new Doppler radar, a lightning detection and display system, a meso-net system and even better computers. We developed and installed a sophisticated, yet user friendly software model for the atmosphere around Kwajalein. The Kwajalein Weather Station became one of the most capable and cost effective military weather facilities in the world.

Reentry Environment Measurements Program (REMP)

The defense buildup of the early Reagan years led to increased funding for tests of both offensive and defensive missile systems. Both the Navy and Air Force were planning tests at Army Missile Range at Kwajalein. I began a campaign to reestablish the REMP Learjet capability.

I urged both the Navy Trident Missile Program and the Air Force Ballistic Missiles Organization to include in their test plans the documentation of clouds through which their reentry vehicles would travel upon reentry. The Navy had always been tough to sell, but eventually was the first to promise funding.

I proposed to equip a Learjet 36 with the particle measurement probes we had used in the late 1970s plus the new Airborne Cloud Characterization Radar (ACCR) that we had developed under Ballistic Missile Organization funding. It had been 5 years since we had used the cloud measurement instrumentation on a Learjet. The equipment was outdated. The engineers and meteorologists who operated the equipment in the previous REMP missions had been laid off years before. I was the only one on our staff who had any experience with it. We needed time to get ready for flight tests.

Unfortunately, the Navy waited until only 2½ months before the first Trident tests was scheduled. The task ahead of us to be mission ready was enormous, considering the short time available, the state of the equipment and the need to train new personnel.

My first problem was to acquire a Learjet 36. Our net worth was not sufficient to finance an aircraft costing upwards of $1.5 million. I had to try for a lease or owner financing. I contacted every owner of a Learjet 36 in the world, seeking a lease or sale with owner financing.

I found one good Learjet 36 at Duncan Aviation, Lincoln, Nebraska. In return for my paying too much for it, Duncan would do a lease-purchase with a guaranteed buyout at the end of the six month lease. I was betting that I would be financially able to buy the plane at the end of the six month lease. Everything depended on my finding other work for the plane during the six months of the Navy contract.

I had to quickly build a team that could pull the instrumentation out of storage and install it on the Learjet, hopefully with a few badly needed improvements. Good performance on the Navy missions was essential to any follow-on business. Jim Matheny, an electrical engineer, had joined us, but had no concept of how the REMP equipment operated. It was a very busy and stressful time but I had to find time to personally direct the reinstatement of the REMP Learjet. With very long work hours, some luck and a one month slip in the Navy test schedule, we were able to hire and train people and get the plane mission ready. We were able to document the cloud environment for the two Navy missions. Our customer was very happy.

By August 1985, I was convinced that the Strategic Defense Initiative Organization (SDIO) would soon have a requirement for optically tracking and photographing missiles from aircraft. I believed that requirement would be a good source of follow-on business for the REMP Learjet. With my increasing confidence, I was able to secure a loan to buy the aircraft at the end of the 6 month lease. However, all future work for it was still a bird in the bush.

With the success of the initial two Navy Trident tests, we were able to secure funding for two additional Navy tests scheduled for mid 1986. BMO also began serious plans to use the Learjet for a series of reentry tests, starting in 1986. I soon realized that I had not only secured the Learjet funding for the near term, but I had over committed it.

Airborne Optical Measurement Systems

By mid 1985, the newly- formed Strategic Defense

Initiative Organization. SDIO was planning its first missile intercept experiment at Kwajalein. They were worried that the usual cirrus clouds would defeat the ground based optical tracking systems that were vital to the experiment. Success of the first mission was considered critical to the future of the whole concept of strategic defense. It was essential that they have good photographic coverage to prove to the Congress that an operational kinetic kill capability was feasible.

I presented a briefing, showing that cirrus coverage at Kwajalein is so pervasive that optical sensors on airplanes above the clouds would be required to get the pictures they wanted. I convinced them that optical tracking systems in aircraft that could climb above the cirrus was the key to their program's success. I believed that airborne optical systems would be a major new market for Aeromet.

I briefed the SDIO folks on my experience in the HOE optical coverage and suggested that we could provide the airborne optical data that they would need. I suggested a gyro stabilized platform so that narrow field-of-view cameras could be used while keeping the target image steady in the picture. The narrow field of view would require a computerized pointing system to locate and track the targets. I suggested that we could use the REMP Learjet because it could get above the cirrus clouds. I was asked to come back in a week with a detailed briefing on how we would do it.

I developed a plan that took the best parts of the airborne and ground based optical tracking systems that I was aware of. My concept required that radar target track files would be telemetered to the aircraft to tell us where the targets were. A computer would generate target pointing angles relative to the aircraft while correcting for turbulence and aircraft maneuvers. I specified a gyro-stabilized mirror that would be positioned by the computer so as to deflect light from the target into a seven inch aperture telescope. The captured light would be split into two paths to feed two or more cameras. Video camera data would be recorded on broadcast quality video recorders. I suggested that a large optical window could be mounted in the existing escape hatch and we would install a new escape hatch in place of the forward right side window. The escape hatches would provide viewing ports for two stable optical platforms, driven by a single computer. Two operators would be ready to take over manual tracking after the targets became visible. My briefing appeared to go very well.

My proposal was accepted, but there were substantial bureaucratic problems in getting the task added to our existing REMP contract. Vic Puckett, our REMP contract technical monitor, came up with an innovative interpretation of one clause in our REMP contract and used it to authorize Aeromet to perform airborne optical measurements. In my entire career in government contracting, I never found any other civil servant to match the get-it-done attitude of Vic Puckett and Barney Davis, his boss. It was lucky for the government, as well as Aeromet that we worked for them at that critical time. The contract modification was done and we were authorized to proceed.

As we began developing our design for the optical system, Barney Davis called to say that Col. John Otten, Director of the new SDIO Mobile Sensors Office was coming to check us out. He warned me that Col. Otten had a reputation for eating contractors for breakfast. Col. Otten spent the day looking over our work, our plant and talking to me. At the end of the day, he told me he believed we could install anything on an aircraft and make it work, but he didn't think we knew beans about optical systems. He said he came prepared to stop what we were doing, but stated he liked what he saw and would continue funding for us if we would get somebody on board who knew optical systems. However, he would cover his bet by developing his own airborne optical system on an Air Force C135. It would be the primary sensor. We would be considered as a backup sensor. I knew we had barely passed a critical test in the development of our optical systems business.

By the fall of 1985, it became clear to me that the mission schedule for the REMP Learjet had become so busy that it would not be able to share time with the optical system requirements. I proposed a second Learjet to be dedicated to optical requirements. The first mission for the second Learjet would be SDIO's Delta 180 mission, scheduled for mid June 1986. It involved one satellite chasing   another and colliding with it at very high speed. We would need two tracking systems in order to track both satellites as they approached the impact point.

In early January 1996, I finally won recognition of the fact that a second Learjet would be necessary to meet mission demands. Barney Davis and I were able to persuade Col. Otten to fund it. After intensive negotiations with Contracts, I was able to get a further modification of our existing REMP contract to provide for a second Learjet. I was not able to finance the purchase of a Learjet at that time, so I had to find an aircraft I could lease. The search was made very difficult by the fact that I planned to make extensive and permanent modifications to the airframe. I had to settle for leasing a Learjet 35, which was like the Learjet 36, but with about an hour less fuel. That made ferry flights to Kwajalein risky and more dependent on favorable winds.

Our development schedule was extremely aggressive. Two groups that had built less complex airborne optical systems than ours had told us it could not be done in less than two years. We had to be mission ready in seven months. I had to hire more engineers and technicians and organize them into teams. The teams included aircraft modifications, stable platform, optical systems, computer systems and software development. I tried to instill a strong sense of urgency and

The HALO I Gulfstream with internal camera systems became the main source for missile test data for the united States.

mission importance on everybody, including subcontractors. I fired one subcontractor who didn't understand the message and took their task in house.

Our biggest challenge was the success-oriented development schedule. The aggressive schedule that I put us on meant many long days for everybody. We could not afford for any team to fall behind schedule. The gyro-stabilized mirror, which was manufactured in Scotland, was a considerable schedule risk. I called on the influence of SDIO to persuade the subcontractor to deliver on our time scale. The software development and integration of the computer-stable platform systems carried the most risk of being late or the system not working. We got lucky - the Delta 180 mission date slipped to September 1986. We were flying the system by mid June and were able to work the bugs out of the systems. By mission date, much to the relief of SDIO, we were ready. We named the system the High Altitude Learjet Observatory (HALO).

We were successful beyond anyone's dreams on the Delta 180 mission. The mission itself was very successful and we did a terrific job in acquiring and tracking the satellites up to a spectacular intercept. Our pictures

The HALO II, with its large telescope mounted atop the fuselage, set the standard for accuracy and sensitivity in optical missile tracking.

were eye-popping. We had just passed another major

milestone in our efforts to become a player in the airborne optical systems market. We were able to parlay that success into further development of the HALO optical system and many more missile tracking missions. Over the next several missions, we developed a reputation for always getting the data, no matter what problems developed. We were told that our competitor, Col. Otten's Air Force C135, called Argus, collected good data only about 25% of the time. Perhaps the highest compliment we could have received came from Col. Otten. During a data review meeting, he told the Argus folks to look at the way Aeromet went about doing the job and do it the same way.

In early 1986, the Army HEDI Program Office awarded a contract to a small Huntsville company to develop an airborne infrared optical system, called the InfaRed Instrument System (IRIS). I was able to win the job to furnish an aircraft for it. That would be our third Learjet in less than a year. I managed to solve the Contracts problem again with a combination of persuasion and some hard ball. I still didn't have the capability of buying another Learjet, but I was able to lease a Learjet 36, once again with the intent to do major modifications on the airframe.

By 1987, we were feeling intense competitive pressure from Argus, Col. Otten's pet Air Force optical systems aircraft. Argus was a HUGE plane, and could carry large aperture optical systems and a large crew. We were considered as skillful and reliable data providers, but the optical systems we could carry in the Learjet were considered too small by some data customers for upcoming missions. I was afraid our optical systems business was doomed unless we could somehow move to a bigger airframe.

I developed a concept for a large aperture open port optical system that could be carried on a Gulfstream II I worked out most of the design problems for a large stabilized mirror operating through a large opening on the side of a Gulfstream II with a compensating pressure vessel structure inside the airframe. I briefed my ideas for the large aperture open port system to all potential customers who would listen. After two years of briefings, I started making headway.

By 1989 the IRIS had outgrown the space available in the Learjet 36. I shifted my strategy from the large aperture optical system to a concept of a Gulfstream IIB that would serve both the HALO optical systems and the IRIS. I finally won an invitation to present my concept to Col. Ross at SDIO. My briefing to Col. Ross went very well and he bought the concept on the spot. We had just passed another critical milestone that was required to stay in the airborne optical systems business.

Our successes over the past four years had improved our financial capability to the point that I could finance an $8 million aircraft and an extension on our hangar to house it. With that deal, I owed over $10 million, all of it depending on short term contracts that could be cancelled at any time we failed to perform. I knew I was playing for high stakes where good performance was critical.

We were able to significantly upgrade the capabilities of our optical systems while we made the transition from the two Learjets to the Gulfstream IIB. We managed to make the transition in ten months, another record time for such a project. We were able to make continuous upgrades as the Gulfstream version of the HALO continued enjoying success as an airborne optical tracking and documentation platform during the 1990s.

By 2000 I had relinquished most operational control to my son, Garry. The company continued growing. The company proposed a second Gulfstream based airborne optical system in 2000. This time, it involved the larger aperture that I had tried to develop in the late 1980s. However, instead of the open port in the side of the aircraft, the design involved placing a 35 cm aperture system on top of the aircraft. It was protected by a pod with a port that could remain closed until the aircraft climbed to clear air on top of all clouds, thereby protecting the delicate optical systems in the pod. The open port could be rotated so the field of view could be moved from either side over the top to the other side, thus greatly increasing the mission flexibility. Once the proposal was accepted, I bought a second Gulfstream II, which we named the HALO II. The HALO II system became one of the most sensitive and accurate optical tracking systems ever devised.

Special Mission Aircraft

In 1985, I heard about a McDonnell Douglas Aircraft Corporation (MDAC) requirement for an aircraft to test two experimental radars. Two MDAC subcontractors were competing for a contract to build a radar that would fit on the nose of reentry vehicles, look at the terrain upon reentry, compare the radar image with a stored image map and steer the reentry vehicle to its target with deadly accuracy. The two proof of concept radars were to be flown on an aircraft to compare their performance.

I proposed a Falcon 20 as the best candidate for their job. We won the competition. As we began working with MDAC engineers, they seemed to recognize that we could do things faster and cheaper than they could, so additional work was added to our contract. We built a rather complex belly-mounted pod to house the two competing radars. The pod had to be environmentally controlled and provide for a host of cameras and other special devices required by the competing subcontractors. We flew the Falcon for MDAC for about two years. It was a very successful project.

The Learjet factory handed off to Aeromet a contract to modify a Learjet 36 to provide for an interferometric synthetic aperture radar (IFSAR) for the Environmental Research Institute of Michigan (ERIM). We built and certified the largest radome ever for a Learjet. It is still flying today.

Another special mission aircraft involved modifying our Cessna 421 to support development of a smart glide bomb. Loral Defense Systems was the prime contractor and our customer. We installed the smart front-end of the bomb on the belly of the 421. The weapon was finally upgraded with a tiny jet engine that would allow the seeker to fly around a target area until it found the type of target that it was programmed to kill. With the growth of the weapon and its test monitoring systems, we needed a larger aircraft. I bought a Cessna Conquest II and we switched the payload to it. Near the end of the program, we were dropping live bombs off of the Conquest onto targets such as tanks or trucks. I believe we had the only Cessna bomber in existence.

Linda and I flew to Zurich, Switzerland to purchase a Cessna Caravan for use by Raytheon to test an experimental mine field mapping system. We flew the Caravan across the Atlantic, contending with airframe icing along the way. We modified the aircraft to accommodate the Raytheon minefield mapping hardware, and then we furnished flight services for a year of testing.

I bought two aircraft, a Gulfstream II and King Air 100, and related contracts from Petersen Aviation, a competitor, in early 1996. The King Air 100 served as a test platform for Interstate Electronics, Inc. to develop a flight management system. The Gulfstream II served as a test platform for development of an autonomous precision landing system being developed by Lockheed Martin. We performed the required aircraft modifications and flew the experimental aircraft for the customer's test flights over about a two year period.

At one point, I owned 11 aircraft, most of which are used as special missions aircraft.

Fixed Base Operations - AVTEC

In moving from Norman to Tulsa in 1977, we gave up a convenient base for aircraft operations. Norman's Westheimer Field. There, we had adequate hangar and office/shop space available. In Tulsa, we were unable to find suitable office and shop space. We rented a small building about 20 minutes from Tulsa International and had to make do with a rented corner of a large hangar for work on our aircraft. We had no space to store tools or equipment. It was a very inefficient arrangement. The sudden downturn of our business with the loss of BMO funding in 1980 made it impractical to buy or build better facilities.

By early 1983, I had realized that there would again be a market for airborne systems tests because of the Reagan-inspired defense buildup. I began a serious search for a suitable airport facility. I heard about a fixed base operation at Riverside Airport on the southwest side of Tulsa being for sale.

I organized a new company, Avtec Services, Inc. to buy the building and the fixed base operation housed in it in March 1983. A fixed base operation (FBO) is a business that furnishes aircraft services to the flying public, including maintenance, charter aircraft, flight training and fuel sales. The FBO was losing money when we bought it. The losses continued in spite of my best efforts to correct it, so I began phasing out of the FBO business. I wanted to use the building as the base for our defense contracting business, which I believed would soon grow again. We did retain a capability for fuel sales and aircraft maintenance to support our own aircraft.

By 1989, we again needed more space. Bill Watts offered to sell his FBO business and building to us. I bought a money-losing FBO business for the second time. My daughter, Karen, took the job of turning the business around. Ultimately, we were unable to turn the business around. We started phasing out of the FBO business in 1994. After years of losses and frustrations, we ceased all FBO operations in 1996 and leased our fuel farm and self service fuel facility to Bill Christiansen, our main competitor. The FBO business was one of my biggest business mistakes. None of it was fun and it seriously detracted from more enjoyable and profitable businesses. We lost over $1 million during 12 years in the FBO business.

PROFESSIONAL AND EXTRACURRICULAR ACTIVITIES

Krick and his Cronies

One day in 1972, I received a call from the Lawton City Manager. He said the Lawton City Council had directed him to let a contract for cloud seeding to fill two reservoirs used by Lawton for city water. Lawton, like many other small western Oklahoma towns, had contracted with Dr. Irving P. Krick to seed clouds for many years. The City Manager's problem was that he had heard enough about Dr. Krick to be suspicious. He wanted me to come to Lawton and talk to him and the City Council about the science of cloud seeding.

I considered Krick to be a complete fraud. He was a distinguished looking man and an eloquent and persuasive speaker. In his magnificent sales pitch he claimed that his forecasts helped win World War II, then he sailed through a little pseudo-science about cloud seeding and wound up with the tremendous economic benefits of green grass and full reservoirs that only he had the power to produce. He made his cloud seeding sound so good and the cost so small for each farmer that they eagerly paid it.

When I answered the Lawton call, I explained that I was in command of the scientific facts, but was no match for Dr. Krick in moving small town audiences. I suggested that if they are bound to spend money on cloud seeding, they should at least look at other alternatives. I suggested two other commercial seeders who had better scientific credibility and certainly a better reputation for scientific honesty than Dr. Krick.

After a few days he called me back. He said he had called Dr. Archie Kahan at the Bureau of Reclamation and asked what the difference between Dr. Krick and me was. He said Dr. Kahan, who had once worked for Krick, told him the difference was that I would tell him the truth. He pleaded with me to come to Lawton to talk to the City Council about cloud seeding. He led me to believe I would be the only speaker in attendance.

When I arrived at Lawton, I found Newt Stone, Krick's right hand man there. The meeting was, in effect, a debate about cloud seeding before the City Council. Newt knew his story well, but did not have the persuasive magic of Krick. I won the debate, at least for that day.

The editor of the Lawton Constitution asked for an interview after the meeting. I repeated some of the same things I had told the council. I was surprised when I got a copy of his editorial in the next issue of the paper. He turned everything I said around and made me out to be a liar and a scientific snob who didn't care anything about the people of western Oklahoma. I later learned that he had been a disciple of Krick for years.

I soon learned that Dr. Krick was closely tied to Ferdie Deering, Agriculture Editor of the Daily Oklahoman and to Governor Hall. I had taken on a battle with some powerful opponents. Ferdie Deering and the Daily Oklahoman continued supporting Krick and putting me and other atmospheric scientists down with cartoons and editorials written by Ferdie. Many small town editors slavishly copied the Daily Oklahoman's line. I continued to battle them for years, but   that was one battle I lost decisively. Krick continued in business for several years.

Weather Modification Policy

During the Krick battles, I became more convinced that there was a need for a national policy on weather modification. In a speech to an American Meteorological Society meeting in Miami in 1983, I took the position that having so many interest groups pulling in opposing directions was defeating a potentially very beneficial national capability. I contended that all interest groups would be better off if we could develop a credible national policy on weather modification and all support that policy. I suggested that national legislation was needed to develop such a national policy. The reaction was agreement in principle, but little enthusiasm for doing anything about it.

At that time, I was serving as the President of the Weather Modification Association which was made up of persons who were engaged in research or operations related to weather modification. I made the same speech to the WMA. The response of most WMA members was that something like my proposal was needed, but there was no ground swell of interest in doing anything to promote it.

In spite of a lukewarm response to my proposal, I decided to try to lead a campaign to develop a national weather modification policy.

I attended a hearing on water resources conducted in Oklahoma by Senators Bellmon of Oklahoma and Dominichi of New Mexico. After the hearing, I had an opportunity to talk to Senator Bellmon about the need for a weather modification policy. He was immediately supportive. He said that, as a farmer, he was keenly aware of the value of a little more rain or less hail, and he had heard enough controversy on the subject to know something should be done to straighten out the mess. He suggested I put my ideas on paper and send it to him. At my request, he sent me copies of a couple of bills he had introduced earlier. I read them carefully to get a feel for how his office wrote bills. I wrote out my thoughts as Senator Bellmon had suggested.

My plan was to get a bill passed that would authorize a board to make a detailed study of all aspects of weather modification and to write a statement of national policy on weather modification. That policy would then become the basis upon which funding for the federal agencies and aid to the states would be based. I had in mind the centralization of authority in one federal agency for all weather modification research and support for operations within the United States. As a minimum, I wanted to set up a formal mechanism for coordinating activities between federal agencies and to give a voice for the universities, the private sector and the user groups in government policy decisions.

As I formalized my ideas, I began seeing how I could write them into the format provided by earlier Bellmon bills. I spent many late evening hours at home working over my typewriter, writing and correcting drafts. When I was finished, I had written my concept into a bill with the legal buzzwords and structure contained in Bellmon's earlier bills. The purpose of the bill was to authorize and fund an Advisory Board on Weather Modification. I wrote the bill so as to authorize a Weather Modification Advisory Board which would be appointed by the Secretary of Commerce and required the Secretary to make a formal report to the President and the Congress. I mailed the draft bill to Senator Bellmon with a letter saying I had taken the liberty of writing my views in the form of a draft bill. I hoped he would be able to use parts of what I had written to develop a bill along those general lines. He wrote back, thanking me for the draft and said he was sending it on to his legal staff for comment.

The next letter from the Senator contained a copy of the bill he proposed to introduce for my comment. To my surprise, only a few words of my draft had been changed, and they did nothing to change the provisions of the bill. I quickly wrote back with my grateful approval. He introduced the bill.

I soon learned that the introduction of a bill means very little. Thousands of them are introduced every year but few ever have hearings and fewer still are reported out of committee. Only a very small percentage of bills introduced ever become law.

The next big job was to develop political support for holding a hearing on the bill in both the Senate and House. It was not hard to get people in the various   interested groups to agree that

135

the Bellmon Bill seemed like a good idea. It was much harder to get people to actually lobby for hearings on the bill. I had to do most of it myself.

I traveled, at my own expense, to Washington several times to lobby for hearings on the Bellmon Bill, first in the Senate then in the House, where Congressman Wes Watkins was kind enough to introduce the Bellmon Bill. I was surprised how hard it was to get the Weather Modification Association to act, even though I had just finished a term as its President. Bob White, Administrator of the National Oceanic and Atmospheric Administration, showed no interest in the bill until he began to realize that it had a serious chance to pass. I finally pressured enough people with an interest in it to write letters or make calls or visits urging hearings on the bill. Once hearings were scheduled, it was easy to get people to testify in order to protect their own self-interest. The testimony was universally in favor of passing the bill. The hearings were successful and we got the bill before both houses for a vote, and it passed easily in both houses. President Ford signed it into law in1976.

The new law required the Secretary of Commerce to appoint a Weather Modification Advisory Board (WMAB) to conduct an assessment all-important aspects of weather modification, including the state of the science and potential for good and harm. The Secretary appointed Mr. Harland Cleveland as its chairman, so the board was usually referred to as the Cleveland Committee. I was one of 18 people appointed to the board. Board members were appointed from each of the perceived constituencies. We met in Washington for an organizational meeting at which Henry Bellmon spoke. We scheduled hearings at approximately six-week intervals at many places around the country. We heard testimony from each federal agency with an interest in weather modification, many state governments, environmental concerns, agricultural and water resources interests, commercial cloud seeders and cloud research experts. We developed a plan for centralizing control of weather modification within the federal government. NOAA and the Bureau of Reclamation competed for our attention in that regard. We developed a report that gave a rather detailed plan for research, operational weather modification, controls to protect the public interest and funding for research, control and licensing.

Our report became a benchmark reference for all aspects of weather modification and became a model for state and federal actions related to weather modification. Several states used our report as the pattern for their own weather modification policies. Working with the Oklahoma Water Resources Board, I developed a weather modification plan for Oklahoma based almost entirely on our WMAB report.

The WMAB policy statement was my greatest accomplishment in the political arena.

American Meteorological Society

Earlene and I became good friends with Dr. Ken Spengler, Executive Director of the American Meteorological Society when I wrote my paper on television weathercasting in 1962. After that, we always attended the annual meetings, which were held in New York City then. In 1964, as Earlene and I checked in for the annual meeting, I heard that the chairman of the AMS Board on Professional Ethics, Dr. Richard Schleusener, was looking for me. He said he wanted to nominate me for membership on the AMS Board on Professional Ethics. I was already serving on the Cloud Physics Committee, but I agreed. The appointment was for five years. The Board on Professional Ethics was one of the governing boards of the AMS. The role of the Board was to consider matters of policy on professional ethics, to investigate breaches of the AMS Code on Professional Ethics and to recommend actions to the AMS Council.

I was soon assigned to investigate a charge of breach of the ethics code by two cloud seeders, Tom Henderson and Ben Livingston resulting from their lawsuits against each other. I flew to Alamosa, Colorado, the scene of the dispute and interviewed members of the public who had knowledge of the dispute. After gathering data, I called the two cloud seeders for a meeting at Norman, Oklahoma. I reviewed the facts as I found them and asked for their responses. They were ready to fight at the beginning of the meeting, but we reached a compromise agreement between them and they shook hands. They didn't like each other any better, but the dispute was settled without resorting to action at the Council. My chairman told me that a dispute had never been settled that way before.

I was later assigned to investigate Harry Geist, a protégé of Dr. Irving P. Krick, a man I was to get to know well and like very little. Ethics charges had been filed against him to the effect that he was fraudulently charging money for specific weather forecasts for stated dates and places more than a year in advance. My investigation found that indeed he was making such forecasts from his living room, with little or no weather equipment and with no scientific basis whatsoever. Everything he was doing was clearly outside the bounds of official AMS policy, the AMS Code of Ethics and against common sense. I talked to him about his actions and learned that he would not apologize or repent in any way. I saw no choice but to put forward a case for dismissal on the grounds of violation of the AMS Code of Professional Ethics to the AMS Council. When I did, Harry sent word that if action was taken against him, he would sue the AMS, its council members and me as individuals. He let it be known that the large TV station for which he did weather broadcasts would also sue and would fund him in any lawsuits. Faced with such a threat, the Council backed down, even though they all agreed that this was the clearest case of breach of ethics ever brought before the Council. I told the Council that if they backed down on this case, the Code should be scrapped and we should write a weaker code that we were prepared to defend.

About that time, I was appointed as Chairman of the Board on Professional Ethics. The Council asked me to follow my own suggestion and to develop a draft of a new Code. I appointed a committee made up of a cross section of the Society to help draft the new Code. The biggest point of controversy was the clause dealing with competition. The old code held that a member may not compete with another member on the basis of price. My conclusion was that the clause could not be defended in court and, if the council were ever forced to take action on the basis of the clause, they would back down because of the prospect of defeat in the courts. Our new draft removed the clause, along with other changes to more properly align the Code with the changes that were being made by other professional societies.

The Council circulated the new Code to key members before putting it to a formal vote by the membership. Some older consulting meteorologists screamed foul when they saw that we had dropped the prohibition against competing on the basis of price. The Council rejected the Code change. About five years later, Dr. Joel Myers, the young forecaster that I had given my ski slope forecasting business to, sued the AMS over the clause in the Code that prohibited competition on the basis of price as being anti-competitive. The AMS lost the case and had to pay out $1.5 million plus legal costs. The Council finally submitted for a vote by the membership the changes to the Code that I had proposed years earlier. It passed. I was sorry I had not fought harder to change the code before the lawsuit.

In 1969, I passed the oral and written examinations required for a Certified Consulting Meteorologist. This certification is similar to a Certified Public Accountant or Registered Professional Engineer, except that it had no legal status with state governments at that time. I would later have a role in giving it legal status. At about the same time, I was given the honor of becoming a Fellow of the AMS, a rare and prestigious honor for any meteorologist.

In 1976, I was appointed to the AMS Board on Certified Consulting Meteorologists. As a member, my main duty was to grade the exam papers of applicants and participate in an oral examination for them. It was a solemn and important charge. Many applicants held the CCM in the same high level of regard as the PhD. The written exam represented an effort equivalent to the CPA or Bar exams.

I became chairman of the CCM Board in 1980. I was disappointed to find that there was a five-year backlog of applications. Some applications had been pending more than ten years. The processing of applications had all but broken down. The CCM program had lost credibility with the certified members and lost its appeal to the membership. A major overhaul was needed. I gathered the entire board at my office in Tulsa and developed a plan that required a strenuous effort by all board members. I wrote over 1300 letters for the board that year. We eliminated the backlog of applicants except for a few who would not respond to our requests for data, and those were later dropped. We developed and documented procedures for timely application processing. The new procedures were incorporated in the charge to future CCM Board chairmen.

I was nominated for a position on the AMS Council and was elected by the membership in 1981. It was certainly an honor to serve on the highest governing body in my profession. I soon found I was dealing mostly with issues of interest to professors and civil servants. I tried to get some issues of interest to private meteorologists before the Council, but with little success. I found little satisfaction in my membership on the Council.

In 1982, Dr. Richard Hallgren, AMS President, appointed me to the AMS Executive Committee. Dick said he was interested in getting a more businesslike management style on the council. I intended to try to increase the role of applied meteorology and private meteorologists in governing the AMS. I played a key role in initiating the Journal of Atmospheric and Oceanic Technology, a new journal on instrumentation, which was important to operational meteorologists. I managed to get a few nominations for positions and awards for private and applied meteorologists.

In 1982, I was asked if I would allow my name to be placed in nomination for President of the AMS. I had almost decided that I was spending too much valuable time with the AMS. I needed to spend that time in our business. However, nomination of a private meteorologist for a leadership role in the AMS was a rare event, so I felt obligated to at least allow my name to be placed in nomination. Besides, I was sure I could not be elected against Dr. Eugene Bierly, a well-known, popular and competent National Science Foundation official. Gene had been in the business of awarding research grants to universities for decades and had a very high approval rating in the university sector. I was right. I finished second - in a field of two. I was not disappointed. If I had won, I would have been obligated to spend large amounts of time on AMS for the next three years.

During that time, it was becoming clear that we had a major opportunity to grow our business because of President Reagan's increased funding for defense. I decided to spend my time on developing the business. I reduced my time spent on professional activities after that.

Scholarships

I have known for many years that I would like to provide scholarships for bright but underprivileged young people with potential to help themselves and others. I wanted to establish a permanent scholarship fund for students who might have proven by hard work and high ethical and moral standards that they are worthy, even though circumstances might have combined to make them seem ineligible for a college education.

In 1995, Linda and I established such a scholarship fund at the Oklahoma State University Foundation. We named the fund the "Diamonds in the Rough Scholarship Fund." The name is derived from Charlie Smith's declaration in 1952 that I was a "diamond in the rough." The fund is endowed at a sufficient level to provide one or two scholarships per year from the earnings. Two students were awarded scholarships in 1996. Several more have followed and are now either in graduate school or serving as productive citizens. Linda and I have also funded scholarships through the Simon Estes Educational Foundation.

In 1997, Linda and I formed our own foundation, called the Booker Foundation, to further establish a permanent means for developing promising young people. The foundation will also serve other worthy causes. It is to be permanently funded from my estate.

Recently, I donated a half section of land that had been appraised at just under a half million dollars to the Oklahoma State University Foundation. It established the Ray Booker Endowed Engineering Scholarship Fund. It's purpose is to provide four or more scholarships to young people who have the desire and talent, but limited means to pursue an education in engineering at OSU.

University

In 1970, I was asked to become an Adjunct Professor of Meteorology at the University of Oklahoma. I did not have time to teach courses, but agreed to serve as a thesis advisor for graduate students who wanted to do a thesis on cloud physics or another discipline with which I was familiar. I invited some students to participate in one of our projects and use the data in their theses. I gave up the Adjunct Professor position when we moved from Norman to Tulsa in 1977.

In the 1980s, I became actively involved with the OSU College of Engineering, Architecture and Technology Advisory Board and have served on its executive committee for a few years. I have been asked to serve on several other similar boards and enjoy the opportunity to help improve the education of young people.

I began making financial contributions to the OSU Foundation in the early 1980s. In 1994, I was asked to serve a term on the OSU Foundation Board of Governors. I found it interesting and rewarding to try to help the university that gave me my start in life. In 1997, I was asked to serve on the OSU Foundation Board of Trustees. I served as Chairman of the Board of Trustees in 2001. We built a new building located at the main entrance to the OSU campus that became the new home of the OSU Foundation during my chairmanship.

Lohmann Medal

Dr. Karl Reid, Dean of the OSU College of Engineering, Architecture and Technology (CEAT) called me early in 1995 to ask if April 7 was open on my calendar - it was. He said I would be at OSU that day being honored as that year's recipient of the Lohmann Medal. I was overwhelmed. The Lohmann Medal was named for the former Dean of Engineering who led the college from relative obscurity to a position of national prominence. The Medal is given annually to a graduate who (supposedly) has distinguished himself through technical achievements. I was sure they had pulled the wrong name out of the Rolodex. How could they give such an honor to a graduate with such a poor school record as mine? He explained that my achievements in airborne measurement systems, including the AURA were what had impressed the selection committee.

I was overcome with emotion at the Lohmann Medal Banquet as they talked about my life from childhood and my professional activities. They had gathered a crowd of about 300 distinguished guests for the awards ceremony. My family was all there. I sat with my Mom, who was the source of whatever strength I had, and my old friend Senator Henry Bellmon, and Dr. L. J. Fila, who had helped me when I struggled in engineering courses. In my acceptance talk, I announced my decision to establish the Diamonds in the Rough Scholarship Fund at the OSU Foundation.

Distinguished Alumni Honors

Another surprise came with a phone call from Penn State, stating that I had been selected as a distinguished alumni and would receive that recognition at ceremonies on September 9, 2000. Linda and I flew to Penn State and I visited the Meteorology School for the first time since I departed 35 years earlier. I was delighted to find that my old thesis advisor and friend, Dr. Charlie Hosler was still active there. I was excited and humbled to be selected for such an honor from so great an institution as Penn State.

Jerry Gill, CEO of the OSU Alumni Association called to say that I would be one of eight receiving a distinguished alumni award for the year 2001. I was even more in awe of this honor because it was OSU that made it possible for me to have a productive career. We were presented the awards at half time in the OSU versus Texas Tech football game on November 10, 2001.

The greatest honor of all came when I learned that OSU would name a new, high-class residence hall after me. Dr. Schmidley, President of OSU, introduced me and presented the award. It included a granite slab with my likeness and a short biographical summary engraved on it. I was honored to have all of my family and many of my friends in attendance for the dedication ceremony on October 11, 2005.

At the dedication of Booker Hall.

FOURTH QUARTER

Transitions

On June 19, 1985 Karen called Earlene, sobbing and saying she thought we had just lost Sabra, our six week old granddaughter. An ambulance had just left, carrying her to the Muskogee Hospital. We rushed to the hospital to find our little girl lifeless in her parents arms. It was my life's harshest blow up to then. That was a time of frantic business activity, and I found it difficult to perform under the load of grief I felt. It was later determined that Sabra died as a reaction to a DPT shot.

Two months after we lost Sabra, we discovered that our son, Larry, had become an alcoholic and desperately needed our help to fight the affliction. We got him into a treatment program near his home in Fort Collins, Colorado. He later moved to Tulsa to be near the support of his family. In March 1988, after years of struggling with alcoholism and numerous treatment sessions, Larry succumbed to his disease. It was a devastating blow to our family. His death came during a long period of stress related to our work. There were times when I sat alone and cried.

In August 1991, Earlene was diagnosed with advanced ovarian cancer. Her surgery and chemotherapy were difficult, but it appeared that her cancer was in remission by January. She resumed her normal life. Her test results continued to be excellent and we began to hope for a cure. However, the cancer returned with a vengeance in May. We made the cruise trip to Alaska that she had wanted to do while we waited for admission to M. D. Anderson in Houston. She lost her battle in September 1992. Our whole family shared her struggle with the disease during her final year.

Earlene had always handled our family finances. I soon found myself struggling with my financial situation. I had to engage a CPA firm to assist me in sorting it all out. I found that I owed back taxes and penalties that I could hardly afford. I was not of sound mind or body following these events. To clear my mind, I spent many hours on my bulldozer, clearing land on the farm.

After a time, I began going out with groups of friends. I hadn't dated anyone in a very long time, so I was awkward in my new social circumstances. Slowly, I began making new friends and became more engaged in social functions.

Linda

Linda Parrish had been a CPA for our companies off and on for twenty years. She left our employment after we lost Metrodata Systems, Inc in 1974. She and her husband, Rick Parrish, moved to Muskogee where they ran a radio station for several years. She began serving as our CPA again while she lived in Muskogee and we were again building a company in the early 1980s. She returned full time to Aeromet in 1987 and eventually moved herself to Tulsa.

Linda and I were married on a beautiful beach on Maui. It was a great start for our marriage.

I had always liked and admired Linda. She was an extremely

dedicated and loyal employee and a dear friend. Our relationship was always strictly professional until after her divorce. Slowly at first, we began having dinner and going to movies. We were alike in many ways and enjoyed doing the same things. We found we both liked ballet, fine music, travel and working with charitable organizations..

After several months, we began to realize that we didn't want to be away from each other. We wanted to be married, but did not want a big wedding ceremony with guests. We settled on a plan to be married in a private wedding at the Kapalua Bay Resort on Maui. It was a beautiful private ceremony by the side of the sea with a bright rainbow as a backdrop. It remains as a beautiful memory for both of us.

We both like flying. As she gained her instrument, flight instructor and commercial ratings and checked out in the helicopter and jets, we began making long and adventurous trips in the Citation, Learjet, Caravan and helicopters.

Linda and I have a happy and successful marriage. She has made me a happy person again.

Business Transition

In 1994, defense budget cuts had placed Aeromet in an extremely competitive environment. Defense contractors were often bidding jobs at a loss just to stay in business. To gain new business in that competitive environment, I believed we needed an extra advantage. That was available in a "8(a)" government program that gave significant advantages to minority-owned businesses. By shifting 51% of Aeromet's stock to Linda, a Choctaw, and making her President, we could qualify for the 8(a) program. I chose to give the other 49% to Garry and made him Vice President for Operations. .

I soon realized my error. The new management arrangement did not work well and it became increasingly dysfunctional. Fortunately, the company continued growing with the development of a second Gulfstream with much higher technology for tracking missiles and characterizing the optical signature from all phases of flights. In 2002, I determined that we would sell the company and Linda and I would retire from it. We closed a sale to L3 Communications, Inc. in May, 2003. We cleaned up the details of the sale over the next 18 months.

When asked if we are now retired, I usually answer that we are not retired, just unemployed. We lead a healthy and active lifestyle. We have enjoyed involvement in charitable activities, including the OSU Foundation, the Tulsa Air and Space Museum, the Simon Estes Scholarship Foundation and the Tulsa Ballet Theatre. We have enjoyed the fellowship with scholars we have sponsored at OSU and OU. We have more time now for our grandchildren.

We expect that there will be more adventures during the remainder of what I am calling the Fourth Quarter of this life. Perhaps more about it will be written when more of it has been lived.

END